REMEMBERING

SINATRA

REMEMBERING SINATRA

10 YEARS LATER

BY ROBERT SULLIVAN

AND THE EDITORS OF LIFE

LIFE Books

EDITOR Robert Sullivan
DIRECTOR OF PHOTOGRAPHY
Barbara Baker Burrows
CREATIVE DIRECTOR Mimi Park
DEPUTY PICTURE EDITOR Christina Lieberman
COPY EDITOR Danielle Dowling

PRESIDENT Andrew Blau
BUSINESS MANAGER Roger Adler
BUSINESS DEVELOPMENT MANAGER Jeff Burak

EDITORIAL OPERATIONS Richard K. Prue,
David Sloan (Directors), Richard Shaffer (Group
Manager), Brian Fellows, Raphael Joa, Angel Mass,
Stanley E. Moyse, Albert Rufino (Managers),
Soheila Asayesh, Keith Aurelio, Trang Ba Chuong,
Charlotte Coco, Osmar Escalona, Kevin Hart,
Norma Jones, Mert Kerimoglu, Rosalie Khan,
Marco Lau, Po Fung Ng, Rudi Papiri, Barry Pribula,
Carina A. Rosario, Christopher Scala,
Diana Suryakusuma, Vaune Trachtman,
Paul Tupay, Lionel Vargas, David Weiner

STAFF FOR THE ORIGINAL 1998 EDITION
EDITOR Robert Andreas
PICTURE EDITOR Barbara Baker Burrows
ART DIRECTOR Samuel J. Serebin
WRITER Robert Sullivan
DEPUTY PICTURE EDITOR Dot McMahon
REPORTERS Priya Giri, Ansley Roan, Pam Stock
COPY EDITOR Melissa Wohlgemuth
PAGE CODERS Larry Nesbitt, Albert Rufino
EDITORIAL PRODUCTION MANAGER
Len Lieberman

TIME INC. HOME ENTERTAINMENT
PUBLISHER Richard Fraiman
GENERAL MANAGER Steven Sandonato
EXECUTIVE DIRECTOR, MARKETING SERVICES
Carol Pittard
DIRECTOR, RETAIL & SPECIAL SALES Tom Mifsud
DIRECTOR, NEW PRODUCT DEVELOPMENT
Peter Harper
ASSISTANT DIRECTOR, BRAND MARKETING
Laura Adam
ASSOCIATE COUNSEL Helen Wan
BOOK PRODUCTION MANAGER Suzanne Janso
DESIGN & PREPRESS MANAGER
Anne-Michelle Gallero
SENIOR MARKETING MANAGER Joy Butts
ASSOCIATE BRAND MANAGER Shelley Rescober

SPECIAL THANKS TO
Alexandra Bliss, Glenn Buonocore,
Susan Chodakiewicz, Robert Marasco,
Brooke Reger, Mary Sarro-Waite, Ilene Schreider,
Adriana Tierno, Alex Voznesenskiy

PICTURE SOURCES
Sinatra memorabilia courtesy of Richard Apt, June
Cook, Nat Dallinger, Bob Foster, Mike Gallagher,
Don Knepp, Maryann Mastrodonato, Ed Shirak Jr.

ISBN 10: 1-60320-012-6
ISBN 13: 978-1-60320-012-7
LOC # 2007910088

"LIFE" is a trademark of Time Inc.

We welcome your comments and suggestions
about LIFE Books. Please write to us at:
LIFE Books
Attention: Book Editors
PO Box 11016
Des Moines, IA 50336-1016

If you would like to order any of our hardcover
Collector's Edition books,
please call us at 1-800-327-6388
(Monday through Friday, 7:00 a.m.–8:00 p.m.,
or Saturday, 7:00 a.m.–6:00 p.m., Central Time).

"Frank Sinatra Has a Cold," copyright 1966,
by Gay Talese, is reprinted by permission
of the author.

MIKE McCANN

SINATRA

FRANK SINATRA WAS AMERICAN CLASSICAL MUSIC'S BEST friend. The great jazz violinist Stephane Grappelli was asked before he died why he never recorded the latest music but stuck to the standards. He replied, "For three hundred years classical music has been Schubert, Brahms, Bach, Beethoven, Mozart. Today's classical composers are Cole Porter, Jerome Kern, Irving Berlin, Duke Ellington, George Gershwin—American jazz. Three hundred years from now this music will still be played."

Sinatra was this music's friend. The '30s and '40s were the golden era of American music, and Sinatra became the music's golden voice. He just drove everybody insane with his talent. He had a musicality that defined the art of intimate singing. He always gave the music his all, and always put integrity before the sound of the cash register.

He was the music's best friend.

And mine as well.

It was my brother, an aspiring opera singer, who told me at the very beginning: "There's this singer, a singer of popular songs. He's really magnificent. His name is Frank Sinatra, and you have to check him out." So I went to see him at the Paramount. I was hooked. I'd catch seven shows a night. Tommy Dorsey was like the Wizard of Oz. He'd have Jo Stafford, the Pied Pipers. He had Ziggy Elman on trumpet and Buddy Rich on drums, all for the admission price of 65 cents. Every one of them would stop the show cold, but when Sinatra hit the stage, he topped them all. No one

could follow him. The audience's reaction was pandemonium. You couldn't get near the Paramount when he was there. It was phenomenal; the streets were all filled up with beautiful girls, thousands lined up for each show.

I was 14 years old. It was still during the Depression, and my father and mother said that if we were going to buy a record, it would have to be one that we'd all enjoy. My family insisted on quality, so all we listened to was Caruso until Sinatra records slowly started to find a place in our home. My favorite record of his is still one of those early ones, "Weep They Will." It's wonderful. I love so many of his songs, but to me it's the best Sinatra record ever. The first lines are "Weep they will, will the lads down the street/When they find that you're promised to me." He did that wonderfully.

The first time I met him was a few years later, after I was established as a successful recording artist in my own right. I was given the summer replacement spot for Perry Como on his *Kraft Music Hall* television show. Since I was still new

To Frank, The ninest friend
I have in the entertainment world.
Thank you   Tony Bennard Benedetto

Horne, Judy Garland, Dinah Washington, Peggy Lee, Margaret Whiting. All these great singers. Fierce competition, but there was a camaraderie. Sinatra was the one who set the tone. We all looked up to him, and he made us feel we were all in it together. He was an inspiration for everyone in show business. Years ago, Frank used to go to Matteo's in L.A. and Patsy's here in New York, and he'd always be the center of attention, the one who made the place come alive. And to this day, in those restaurants, his great friends still show up every Sunday night, and I swear they're waiting for Sinatra to come in. He's the guy who gave us all something to live for.

My favorite quotes about Sinatra are from two of his favorite buddies. Bing Crosby once said, "A talent like Sinatra comes along once in a lifetime. Why did it have to be in my lifetime?" And Dean Martin said, "It's Frank's world, and we just live in it."

He was simply the best. There are a lot of opera singers, but there was only one Caruso. There are a lot of popular singers, but there was only one Sinatra. He was the ultimate pro. Once, when I was in L.A., he invited me to the recording date for the Johnny Mercer song "Summer Wind," conducted by Nelson Riddle. He did it in one take. One take, and Sinatra gets into this gorgeous Italian sports car, rolls down his window and says to me, "Was that all right, kid?" and—*zing*—he drives away. Perfect Sinatra!

You have to understand, in the early days, before electronics, a singer had to sing loud enough to hit the back of the hall. But with the advent of the microphone, everything changed. It allowed the performer to sing intimately. Bing Crosby was the one who taught us how to sing in a conversational way. He was a pioneer. Crosby was the first to expose the listener to what he, the performer, was feeling at that moment. Sinatra expanded on that premise by making

at show business, I was nervous as all heck. I thought I'd take a big chance and seek Sinatra's advice. Sinatra was over at the Paramount, and I decided to visit him backstage. A friend of mine warned me not to go because Sinatra had a reputation for being tough. But I took a deep breath and showed up at his dressing room. The Sinatra I met was quite different from the one I had expected. Sinatra was wonderful to me. I asked him, "How do you handle being nervous onstage?" He said, "It's good to be nervous. People like it when you're nervous. It shows you care. If *you* don't care, why should *they*?" And then he told me to stay away from the cheap songs. It was great advice. I've followed it since.

The competition was intense back then. It was a great era—you had Jo Stafford, Dick Haymes, Nat King Cole, Ella Fitzgerald, Sarah Vaughan, Rosemary Clooney, Louis Armstrong, Billy Eckstine, Lena

WORDS AND PAINTINGS BY TONY BENNETT

the songs autobiographical. Psychologically, he was able to say to himself, "I've lived this, now I can sing it." You could read Sinatra's life through his music. You have to be very brave to sing like that, and it set him apart from all others.

There are many misconceptions about Sinatra. There were certain times in his life when he didn't get proper credit for being the humanist that he was. Not that he asked for credit. But, anyway, I'd like to set the record straight on a couple of things. Sinatra's love affairs were permanent. For instance, there were questions about how much Ava Gardner loved him. Well, she told me that she loved Sinatra just as much as he loved her. His relationships were deep and not frivolous. There was a poetic side to Sinatra that was rarely brought to the forefront.

He was a charitable man. I can't tell you how many times he helped out fellow entertainers who were down on their luck. He never asked for anything in return. He raised more than a billion dollars for charities throughout the world without making a big deal of it.

We never spent as much time together as I would have liked. We both had performance schedules that always had us going to the ends of the earth. And he lived in California, while I was in New York. But whenever we did get together, it was a definite thrill.

I remember many great moments—and funny ones, too. For instance, I was marching to Selma with Martin Luther King Jr., Harry Belafonte and many others, and I noticed Jilly Rizzo, Sinatra's right-hand man, marching next to me. I said, "Jilly, what are you guys doing here?" I looked at him, and I see he's got these brass knuckles on. He's wearing them! And he looks at me and says, "Just in case any of these guys want trouble." And I say, "Jilly, this is supposed to be a peace march!"

A lot of people don't realize that Sinatra was very active in the civil rights movement. But of course everyone *does* know about his relationship with the Kennedys. Through his campaign efforts, Sinatra almost single-handedly got JFK elected. Then Bobby Kennedy advised his brother not to hang around Sinatra anymore. Now, in order to make it easy for Jack to visit, Sinatra had built a whole new section on his house, including a helicopter pad. Then Jack goes off and stays with Bing Crosby. That did it: Sinatra was a Republican before he went to bed. He had a code regarding loyalty that was hard and fast. Once you broke with him, it was over. That was the way he was: If you crossed him, that was it, he didn't even know you.

LOYALTY: That one word overrides anything else you need to know about Sinatra. And of course it worked both ways with him. If he loved someone, he loved them for life. It didn't matter if you were the queen of England or a waiter. If you just said a nice thing about Jilly, for instance, that would get a smile from him. He'd get a kick out of that. He really loved Jilly. The man was full of love. One night my mother and I were watching Sinatra on TV doing *The Main Event.* He knew my mother was dying, and he turned to the audience and said that Tony Bennett was his favorite guy in the whole world. My mother's face lit up like a Christmas tree—this image will stay with me as long as I live. That was the kind

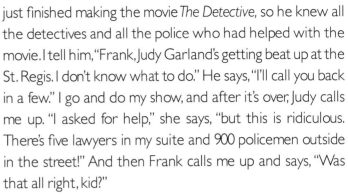

of small thing he would do that would make such a big difference.

And then there was this other night, years ago. It's just moments before I'm about to walk out onstage for opening night at the Empire Room at the Waldorf, here in New York. All of a sudden I get a call. It's Judy Garland. She's on the phone, telling me that she's at the St. Regis Hotel and she's being beaten up—a domestic thing or something. And I don't know what to do. My ex-wife says to me, "Call Frank." He was at the Fontainebleau in Miami. I call him up. He had just finished making the movie *The Detective,* so he knew all the detectives and all the police who had helped with the movie. I tell him, "Frank, Judy Garland's getting beat up at the St. Regis. I don't know what to do." He says, "I'll call you back in a few." I go and do my show, and after it's over, Judy calls me up. "I asked for help," she says, "but this is ridiculous. There's five lawyers in my suite and 900 policemen outside in the street!" And then Frank calls me up and says, "Was that all right, kid?"

He loved doing things like that. Absolutely loved it. It's what he lived for.

Sinatra was like Barrymore. He poured a lot of champagne for a lot of people—and he loved to do the pouring.

When I think of Sinatra, I think of the way that Laurence Olivier depicted Hamlet. He was Everyman. He ran the gamut of emotions. Sinatra conquered every aspect of his world, the entertainment world. He was the two masks of the theater—the comedy, the tragedy. Underneath it all, he was a very, very sensitive, nice person.

Once, I read *The Autobiography of Benvenuto Cellini.* Benvenuto was a sculptor in Renaissance Italy whose works were pure magic. Kings and popes from Italy and France demanded his works. Benvenuto's father demanded true justice from everyone he encountered, and he passed this philosophy down to his son. Benvenuto would draw his sword and battle every hypocrite and phony who stood in the way of truth. It reminded me so much of Sinatra that I once sent a copy of the book to him for his birthday. I inscribed it: "If Shirley MacLaine's philosophy is right, you *must* have been this cat in another life."

Sinatra leaves behind a legacy of music, a legacy that will live forever. Five hundred years from now, people will still be listening to his recordings, watching his films, and they'll say, "There was only one Sinatra." And that's not an opinion, it's a fact.

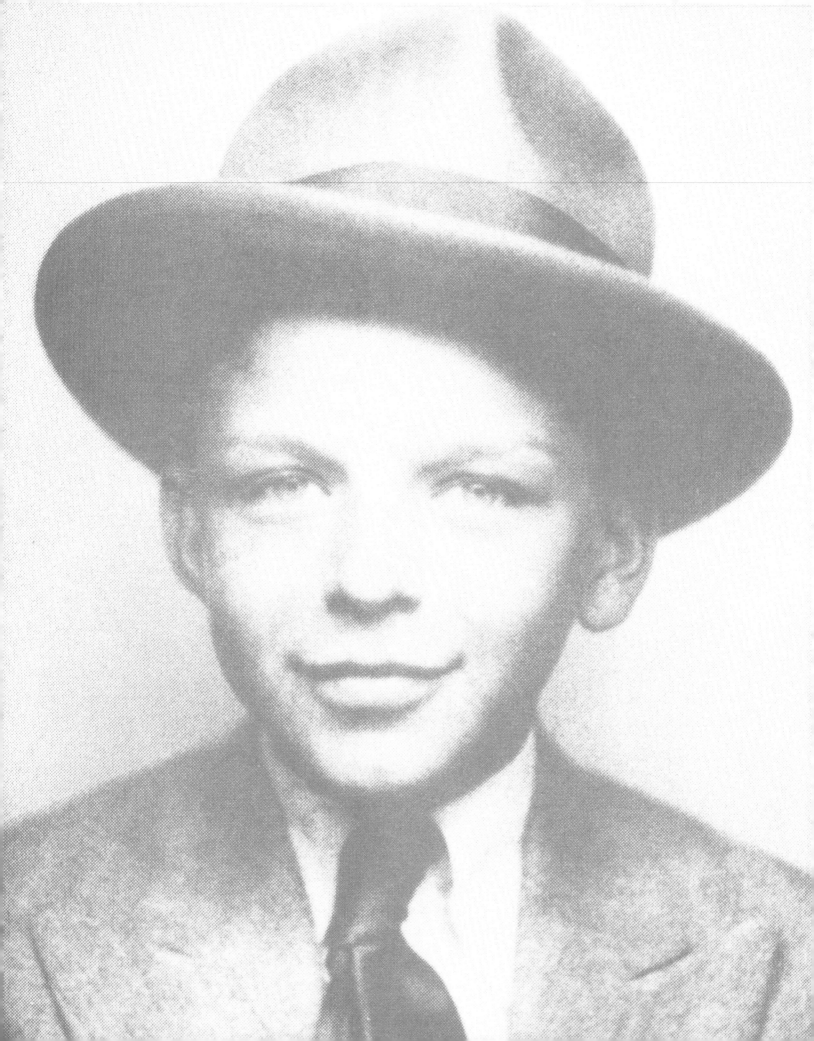

A KID FROM HOBOKEN

Today, you rise from the depths of the train station and step into an old town of red brick and cobblestone. The first thing you notice is the big sign for the Clam Broth House, a restaurant that years ago had another immense sign affixed to its roof, this one proclaiming HOBOKEN: THE HOMETOWN OF FRANK SINATRA.

Well, that was a long time ago. Many moons ago. Many miles.

You drink in the scene, the bustle down by the trains that pull out every 10 minutes and dive under the Hudson River on tracks that represent an umbilical of excitement and possibility, a cord tying this gritty town to Manhattan. You hear the newsdealers hawking their papers, you see the cabbies leaning on their wheels, the cops walking the depot

"My grandmother had more sense than anyone in the room, as far as I was concerned. I have blessed that moment in her honor ever since. Otherwise I wouldn't be here."

Francis Albert, as he always signed his letters to friends, was **outsize from the get-go,** a thirteen-and-a-half-pound baby born to a woman less than five feet tall. The doctor's forceps scarred him for life, leaving their mark on his ear, cheek and neck. Francis's eardrum was punctured during that horrific delivery.

12

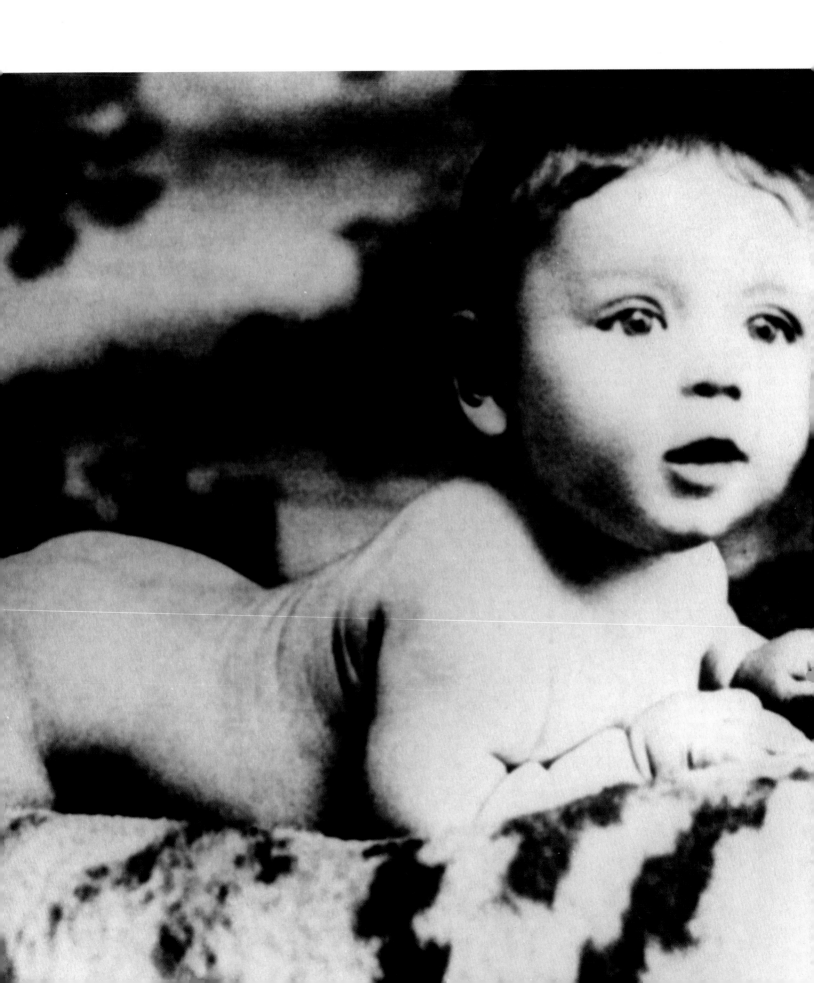

beat in desultory fashion. You figure it must have been pretty much like this.

Two weeks before Christmas of 1915, the snow was blowing hard. Just a few blocks from here, in a cold-water flat at 415 Monroe Street, 20-year-old Natalie Sinatra, famous to all as Dolly, gave troubled birth to a boy. The baby nearly died then and there. Thank God Dolly's mother, Rose Garavente, a midwife of long experience, noticed that the infant wasn't breathing. She grabbed him from the panicking Dr. Peterson and held him under cold running water. Finally, the baby cried out. Sinatra's first note: loud, long, intense, probably on key.

The building on Monroe was torn down years ago. Today, when you visit, you find a gold-and-blue star on the sidewalk outside Pinky's wholesale-and-retail emporium. FRANCIS ALBERT SINATRA, it says inside the star, THE VOICE. And then it says how he was born here on that date, the 12th of December. There's no room to say how he broke out, how he started singing in the local roadhouses for cigarettes—"all night for three packs"—and went on to become the greatest, biggest, brashest, most controversial, most charismatic, most beloved, most detested entertainer the world would see in his century. There's no room, but it doesn't matter. Everyone who comes here knows that already.

His parents (top left) were **Italian immigrants.** Marty was a Hoboken fireman. Dolly was a woman who handed down a fiery personality.

Frank (center) **would have no siblings.** "It was very lonely for me," said Sinatra of being an only child. "Very lonely."

He looked **the little saint** on the day of his First Communion (top right). But he was posing: "Mom kept physically fit chasing me and whacking me around."

The only thing he liked about his school days (opposite) was singing in public. **Expelled from high school,** he never went back and soon was crooning in bars.

On September 8, 1935, Sinatra (opposite, far right) sang as a member of the **Hoboken Four** on NBC Radio's *Major Bowes and His Original Amateur Hour* (that's the Major in the middle). The quartet covered a Bing Crosby–Mills Brothers hit, "Shine," and won the contest: Frank's first break. In his nightclub act in the '60s, Sinatra would remember Bowes as "a pompous bum with a bulbous nose. He used to drink Green River. He was a drunk, this guy. I don't know if you ever heard of Green River, but it takes the paint off your deck if you got a boat. Fifty-nine cents a gallon, baby."

Jersey City's **Nancy Rose Barbato** was sitting on the porch manicuring her nails when Frank fell, hard. At 16, she was his first serious girlfriend; on February 4, 1939, she became his first wife, at age 20. He needed her badly. His father didn't think much of this singing business; Marty figured his dropout son wouldn't amount to anything. Nancy, though, immediately believed in Frank's dream. She was, said Sinatra, "my only escape from what seemed to be a grim world."

A skinny kid on the cusp of something very, very big: Frank was **already getting noticed** by the time he became a father for the first time, in 1940. (Daughter Nancy can be seen opposite and top left with her dad; immediately above with her mom.) These are early fan club shots taken in greater New York and traded by the bobby-soxers there.

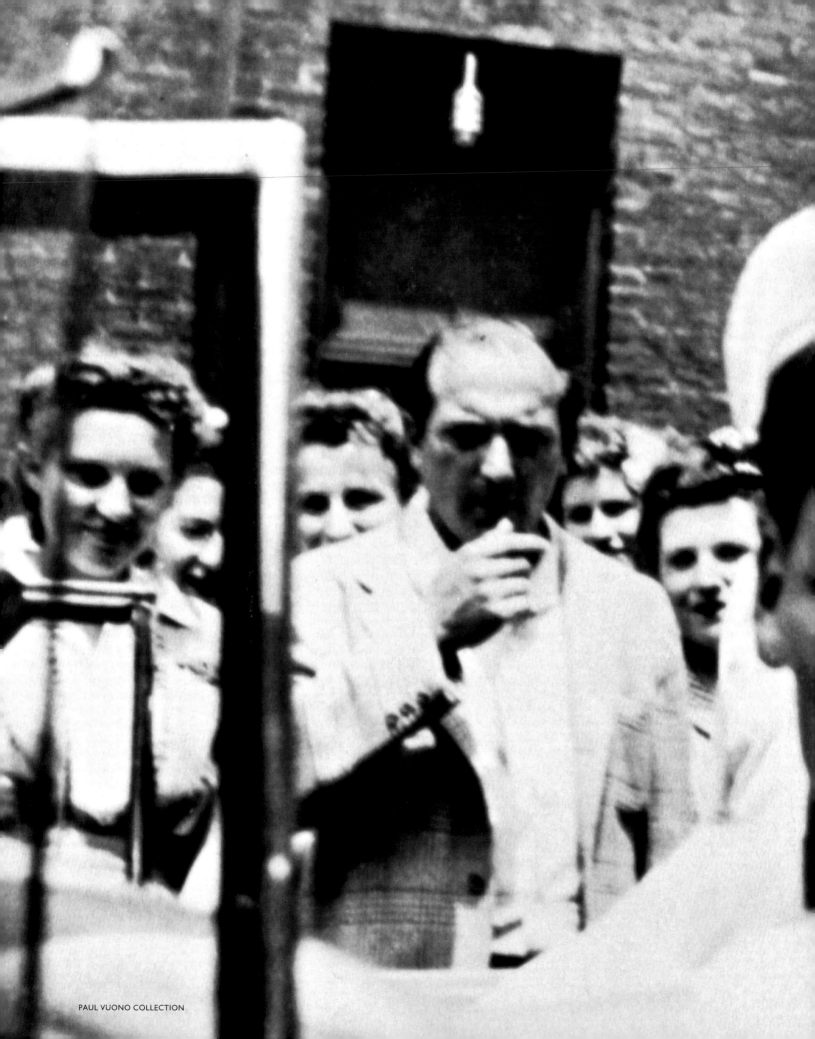

Harry James had caught Frank's act at a joint in Jersey and admired his way of "talking a lyric." Now Hoboken looked on proudly as **Frank started making it,** fronting James's orchestra at clubs and even theaters across the river.

THE VOICE OF FRANK SINATRA

FRANK SINATRA
Vocal
Orchestra under the direction
of Axel Stordahl

TRY A LITTLE TENDERNESS
(Woods - Campbell - Connelly)

36920

C-112-6

COLUMBIA

the voice
of

FRANK SINATRA

orchestra under the direction of
Axel Stordahl

set c·112

you go to my head
don't know why
ese foolish things
ghost of a chance
shouldn't i?
a little tenderness
one to watch over me
ise

PERFECTLY FRANK

15 Songs We Love

Night and Day

All or Nothing at All

Witchcraft

The Lady Is a Tramp

Come Fly with Me

I'll Never Smile Again

I've Got You Under My Skin

How About You?

Angel Eyes

One for My Baby

April in Paris

Autumn in New York

I Get a Kick out of You

Once I Loved

Street of Dreams

15 Songs We Adore

In the Wee Small Hours
of the Morning

Drinking Again

Indian Summer

Moonlight in Vermont

I've Got the World
on a String

I'll Be Seeing You

Put Your Dreams Away

The Song Is You

All the Way

What Is This Thing
Called Love?

From This Moment On

Let's Fall in Love

The Second Time Around

The One I Love Belongs
to Somebody Else

The Music Stopped

5 We Never Play

Mama Will Bark

My Way

Bang Bang

Mrs. Robinson

Strangers in the Night

HENRY GROSKINSKY

23

Walking down Broadway between 44th and 43rd streets today, you pass eateries, a three-card monte stand, eyes-up tourists. In 1943 and '44, walking here, you'd have been forced into the street. The sidewalk would have been packed with thousands of squealing teenage girls, some of them here since sunup, anxious to get into Frankie's next show at the Paramount Theatre.

"Swoonatra" sings "As Time Goes By" at the Riobamba (above), a New York nightclub, soon after his first stint at the Paramount (by then dubbed the Para-Sinatra) had made him a $2,500-a-week sensation. When **The Voice got a throat infection,** he was treated uptown at Mount Sinai Hospital, which became in the papers "Mount Sinaitra."

With several club or theater sets each evening, plus the rehearsals and performances for a new gig on CBS Radio (opposite), he would sometimes sing **a hundred songs a day.** He'd eat half a dozen meals to keep his energy up: "You gotta eat to belt those notes out."

It had already been a heady ride. Yesterday he was singing for 15 bucks a week at a roadhouse called the Rustic Cabin—had to wait tables between sets—and then he gets discovered by Harry James, switches to Tommy Dorsey, and suddenly he's No. 1. Guys had been big before. Rudy Vallee had been big. Crosby was still huge. But now the polls say Sinatra is bigger. He seizes the moment and bolts the Dorsey band. ("I hope you fall on your ass," says Tommy as the door closes.) He gets booked to open for Benny Goodman at the Paramount. The King of Swing doesn't get it. Hit with the scream, Goodman mutters, "What the hell was that?"

That was the beginning. Yeah, sure, Sinatra's manager had spread cash among the first girls in return for some swooning. But once the fire was stoked, it burned on its own—red-hot. Sinatra's swagger trumped Crosby with the thrilling aspect of sex. Only 137 pounds, but Sinatra was all about sex. Too much so for his own good. As his career soared, his home life suffered. Sinatra's handlers did a pretty good job with domestic-bliss publicity shots that seem today like inscrutable artifacts from a bygone era. But within the family, there was pain. Frank's daughter Nancy, always his pet, heard her mother crying behind closed doors: "I would just go away thinking, Mind your own business. Daddy's just on the road again."

26

ABOVE: HERBERT GEHR (3). OPPOSITE: EVERETT COLLECTION

In interviews with LIFE, three who knew him—and *it*—talked about The Voice. **Mel Torme:** What makes for the quality of a singer is the attention to the lyric, extraordinary breath control, perfect intonation, singing in tune and with great feel and understanding for the subject matter. That's what makes a great singer, and Frank was in a class by himself. Bob Eberly was a world-class singer, but I don't think he was on a par with Frank Sinatra. We had a talk one night at Christmas, Frank and me, at his daughter's house. We talked about the three C's: concentration, consistency and credibility. He said: "A lot of us can't sing these tunes that the kids are singing. They're marvelous, but how can we sing these

lyrics?" He stayed credible. **Rosemary Clooney:** All of us bring our own baggage to songs, and so the meaning of a song changes subtly from singer to singer. There was a time when Frank had broken up with Ava Gardner, and everyone was sure that he was singing all those lost-love songs to her. Maybe, maybe not. For me, Frank is woven into the fabric of my life. Incidents that happened, big and small, are instantly recalled when I hear a certain Sinatra song. **Tony Bennett:** Sinatra was a melody man, but melody isn't the whole thing to putting a song across. "The best thing to do is study your music," he told me, "then be yourself. Be yourself. Everybody will like what you're doing if you just be yourself."

WIDE WORLD PHOTOS

At one point during the **height of the frenzy,** grab-happy "Sinatratics" (above) ruined four of Frank's expensive suits in a matter of days. In the '40s, Sinatra's punctured eardrum kept him out of the service, so while older male stars were overseas, the new kid had the female field to himself.

And females of all ages loved him (left, during a taping of the 1940s *Light Up Time* television show). *Time* reported: "**Not since the days of Rudolph Valentino** has American womanhood made such unabashed love to an entertainer." But Sinatra was simultaneously sexy and safe: Since he was famously a father himself, he was family fare.

31

Relaxing backstage at the
Paramount, in a pose not half so
casual as it might appear, Sinatra
already knew at age 29 what
top-of-the-heap felt like.
**"Nobody's ever been a
bigger star than me,"** Frankie
Boy said. "This'll never end."

IKE VERN

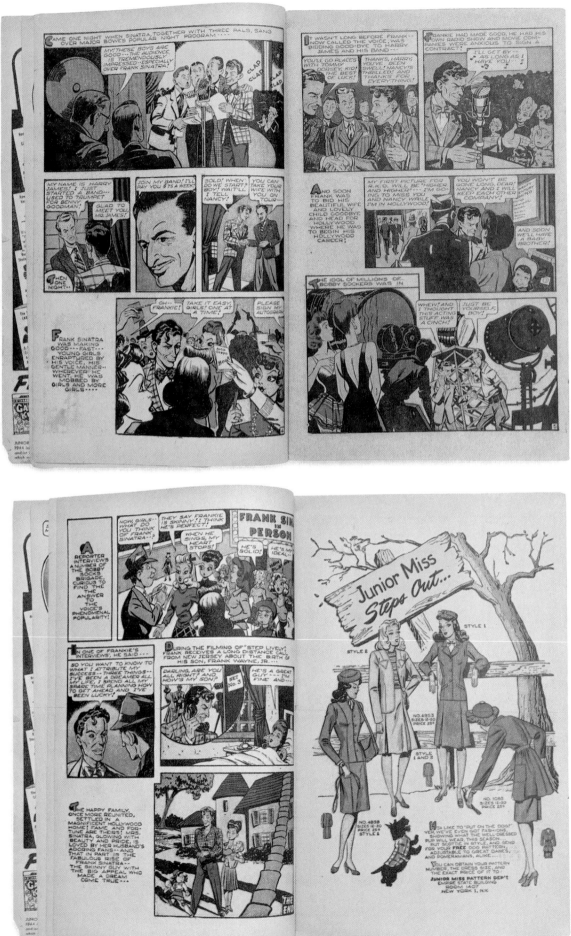

Sinatra's songs and his singing seem so sophisticated today, it's easy to forget that his early fandom was made up largely of 13-to-15-year-old girls. **"I was the boy in every corner drugstore,"** Sinatra said. Of the scores of biographies written about him (only daughter Nancy's accounts were authorized, by the way), this "Life Story," which appeared in the comic book *Junior Miss* in 1944, is among the most charming. The plot moves breathlessly from Frank's days as a cub sports reporter ("Best job a guy ever had!") to the Rustic Cabin, Harry James and Hollywood: "Fame and fortune are theirs!"

Back in the days when Sinatra was hamming it up with Danny Kaye (opposite), The Voice was a silvery tenor. Then it mellowed, taking on the rich hues of all that whiskey. Sinatra wrote in LIFE in 1965: "Over the years my voice has held up pretty good. It's deepened and darkened a bit, which is fine with me, because I used to think it was too high. The only time I ever lost it was in 1949 or 1950. . . . It was in February and I had a real bad cold, and was run down physically—my resistance was knocked out. I came out onstage at the Copa one morning about 2:30 to do the third show. **I opened my mouth, and nothing came out**—absolutely nothing—just dust. I was never so panic-stricken in my whole life.

"Finally I turned to the audience and whispered into the microphone, 'Good night,' and walked off the floor." The doctor diagnosed a vocal hemorrhage and told Sinatra to remain absolutely silent for 40 days: "Toughest thing I ever did."

In 1943, LIFE was complicit in pushing the notion of domestic bliss at Chez Sinatra in Hasbrouck Heights, N.J. But don't think that these photo setups are entirely stuff and nonsense. For instance, Sinatra would spend his life finding and buying the latest phonographic equipment (top left) and listening to and analyzing not only his own music but others'. He could never find enough time for Nancy Jr. (top right, bottom left and far left). And from the time he had two dimes to rub together, he enjoyed playing the gracious and overly generous host, particularly for his male friends and particularly when bottles of hard stuff were involved (bottom right). Later, his Rat Pack pallies, seeing this as his favorite role, would dub him the Innkeeper.

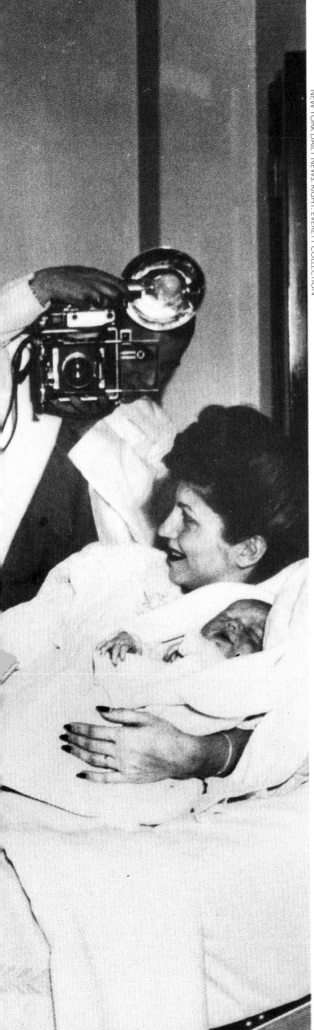

When "Frank Jr." was born in Jersey City, N.J., on January 10, 1944 (left), Dad was a continent away in Hollywood, doing a radio concert. **The boy's name was not Francis** but Franklin, after President Roosevelt. His middle name, Emmanuel, was chosen in tribute to Dad's buddy Manie Sachs—who would later save Sinatra's life.

Sinatra, having missed the births of his two children (above) and with his career now centered in Hollywood, made **a final attempt to save his family:** In 1944 the Sinatras relocated to Toluca Lake, Calif. "We had a kayak and a sailboat and a big raft," Nancy Jr. later remembered. "It was a beautiful life."

Final days of the frenzy: Sinatra was mobbed when he received **the key to the city** of Hoboken in 1947. (The fireman at the bottom of the photo, center, is his father.)

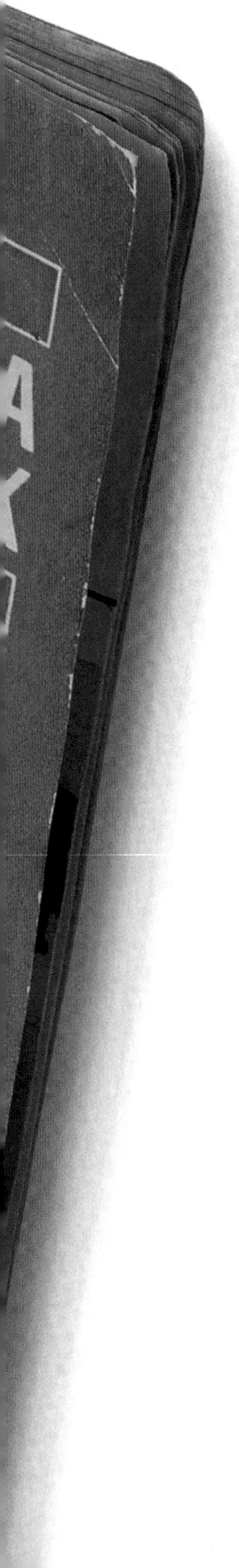

15 Hot Headlines

SINATRA, IN BRAWL,
LOSES TWO TEETH IN LAS VEGAS HOTEL

SINATRA VERSION OF RAID DISPUTED

10 Nicknames We Dig

Ol' Blue Eyes
The Voice
The Chairman of the Board
Frankie Boy
Swoonatra
The Bony Baritone
The Innkeeper
The Swing-Shift Caruso
The Lean Lark
The Groovy Galahad

SINATRA CHASES MOTORIST
AFTER MINOR COLLISION

SINATRA IN CAMERA TUSSLE

"IT WASN'T FRANK'S FAULT AT ALL"

SINATRA SPA IN JAM OVER HOOD

A VIDA TUMULTUOSA DE FRANK SINATRA

SINATRA ROUTS PARISIAN
PHOTOGS WITH FIREWORKS

SINATRA IS ANGRY AT SPANISH COPS

13 Women He Dug

Nancy Barbato*
Marlene Dietrich
Ava Gardner*
Kim Novak
Gloria Vanderbilt
Lauren Bacall
Natalie Wood
Juliet Prowse
Jill St. John
Mia Farrow*
Hope Lange
Victoria Principal
Barbara Marx*

SINATRA, LAWFORD SUED BY DRINKER

SINATRA GETS BOPPED ON HIS NOSE

DESI ISN'T MAD AT FRANKIE,
BUT CALLS HIM "BUM"

SLUGGER SINATRA MIXES
COCKTAILS WITH FISTS

REX HARRISON SLAPS FRANK SINATRA

SINATRA LEARNING TO RELAX

*wives

At Ciros, the Mexican joint at 705 North Evergreen in Los Angeles, you can get a pretty fair enchilada. In 1947, you wouldn't get into Ciro's on Sunset Boulevard (of course), unless you *were* a big enchilada, a very big one indeed. Ciro's was swank. It was the place to be. On a nightly basis, it was where things were happening.

Sinatra walked out of
Beverly Hills Justice Court
(above) after settling with
Lee Mortimer and having his
assault charges dismissed.
Said Sinatra: "I was raised in
a tough neighborhood
where you **had to fight**
at the drop of a hat, and I
couldn't help myself."

Ava Gardner (opposite), on
her days as **the other
woman:** "I didn't
understand then and still
don't why there should be
this prurient mass hysteria
about a male and a female
climbing into bed and doing
what comes naturally."

They were happening big-time on April 8 that year. In this corner of the club was Lee Mortimer, a Hearst enchilada whose beat was gossip. In that corner was Frank Sinatra, still an enchilada supremo in the world of entertainment, but one who was starting to slide. The columnists—Dorothy Kilgallen, Louella Parsons, Hedda Hopper—had been bugging Sinatra lately with their rumor and innuendo. The stuff by Robert Ruark, that business about Lucky Luciano being "Frankie's boyfriend," hadn't gone down well. But it was Lee Mortimer who, on a weekly basis, really got to Sinatra, writing that the busboy could sing better and, what's more, insulting Frankie's fans: "imbecilic, moronic, screemie-meemie autograph kids." Sinatra was already on record: "I will belt him sometime." Mortimer had sent back word that he was ready: "Tell that to him and his cheap hoodlums."

So the temperature in Ciro's that night in '47 was plenty hot. Sinatra noticed Mortimer across the room. Did Mortimer notice him back? Did Mortimer flash "one of those 'Who do you amount to?' looks," as Sinatra will claim? Did Mortimer call him "a dago son of a bitch"? Did Sinatra call Mortimer "a degenerate"? Accounts will vary, as they say. "I followed him out," Sinatra will report, and to this all parties will attest. "I hit him. I'm all mixed up." These things, too, will be conceded, and it will generally be agreed that Mortimer went down hard. The cops caught up with Sinatra later that night at a radio station, and they hauled him into court. Well, this sure wasn't going to make the bad press go away—and things would quickly get worse.

Ciro's vanished years ago, and so did an America that presumed guys like Frank Sinatra were spending time with the wife rather than at Ciro's with, say, Ava Gardner. "People forget the climate in those days when Frank started running around with Ava," remembered Mitch Miller, who was there. "When Sinatra left his wife, the priests told the kids, 'Don't buy his records.'" Today at Ciros, the Mexican place, they'd laugh if you told them Mitch's story.

" I love her. God damn me for it. "

This photo, taken on April 9, 1947, captures a pivotal moment in Sinatra's career. He had risen to the very top and was **about to plummet.** He had punched out Mortimer (at right) and now found himself in court. After his arraignment, Sinatra was told by Louis B. Mayer, his benefactor at MGM, to "settle the damn thing." And so he gritted his teeth, to the tune of $9,000. This didn't necessarily make Mortimer happy, either: Anticipating a long jury trial, he had bought four new suits for his upcoming "personal appearances."

After the money changed hands, Milton Berle told Mortimer, "You're the first fighter to lose a decision and win a purse." Sinatra said defiantly, "It was a pleasure to pay it."

And then it was back to work as Sinatra tried to stop his skid and Mortimer threw oil under his wheels. Who won? One year later, Sammy Davis Jr. noticed his friend "slowly walking down Broadway with no hat and his collar up and not a soul . . . paying attention to him. This was the man who only a few years ago had tied up traffic all over Times Square."

Years after that, Sinatra, loaded, urinated on Lee Mortimer's grave. "I'll bury the bastards. I'll bury them all."

51

Humiliated by Frank's behavior, Nancy filed for separation on Valentine's Day, 1950, and began officially raising the children on her own: "the juniors," Nancy (left) and Frank, plus Tina, who was born in 1948. "When he left home, I was a baby," Tina said later. "I didn't feel the wrench. I didn't know him." The Sinatras, Catholics, didn't divorce until November 1951; Frank married Ava a week later. They sparred constantly, these "Swinging Sinatras." Frank reacted dramatically, then desperately. His **"suicide attempts"** with the gun and the pills were fakes to get Ava's attention. But the night in 1952 when, drunk, he turned on the gas oven and pulled up a chair—that one was very real. He was unconscious when Manie Sachs arrived, saving his life. Gardner left him a year later.

One dark day in the Dark Ages, Sinatra turned to his friend Hank Sanicola and said, "Little by little, man, I'm dying."

53

FRANK
PETER

PANAVISION® TECHNICOLOR®

"SERGEANTS" 3

AVEC HENRY SILVA • RUTA LEE
ECRIT PAR MIS EN SCENE PAR
W. R. BURNETT • JOHN STURGES

54

15 Flicks to Find

On the Town
The Manchurian Candidate
From Here to Eternity
Some Came Running
The Tender Trap
Suddenly
High Society
The Man with the Golden Arm
Pal Joey
Robin and the Seven Hoods
Contract on Cherry Street
The Joker Is Wild
The First Deadly Sin
Von Ryan's Express
Higher and Higher

5 Reel Dogs

The Pride and the Passion
Double Dynamite
Sergeants 3
Johnny Concho
The Kissing Bandit

The Sands, too, is history: the Hoboken house, the Paramount, Ciro's, even the Sands. You may have seen it go down. The big *kaboom* was used in *Con Air,* a movie that didn't feature Sinatra—he was 80—but might have, way back when. It's about a bunch of tough guys hijacking a plane. Can't you see Frank, Dino, Sammy, Peter and Joey? Sinatra's top-billed, of course—Leader of the Pack.

Sinatra got lucky:
His screen test for the
role of Maggio in *From
Here to Eternity* (above and
opposite) was set in a
barroom. Director Fred
Zinnemann said to him,
"Do something. You
know, what does a drunk
do at the bar?" Sinatra had
a pretty good idea.
"Well," he said, "drunks
do a lot of things at bars."
His acting looked
authentic and he got the
part—and the Academy
Award for Best
Supporting Actor of 1953.

Vegas is different these days. You cruise the strip and you're hit with lasers, casinos that look like mini-Manhattans, roller coasters. Kiddie rides. Everything's crowded with all sorts of people, not just gents in tuxedos and ladies in cocktail dresses.

The Sands opened December 15, 1952. That night you could have got long odds betting that a has-been named Sinatra would come back and headline the first big Sands date of 1960 with something called the Rat Pack. You could've cleaned up, betting on Sinatra.

The story's well known: It was the movies—*a* movie—that in 1953 picked Sinatra up and put him back in the race. Did his gangster friends get him the part? Make offers that couldn't be refused? It just shows how Sinatra, even a down-and-out Sinatra, could create American mythology. When it came to Sinatra, you'd believe anything.

Now, Sinatra's hooking up with Nelson Riddle—that was no mob deal. That was kismet, and the boys don't lean on kismet. The Voice was

"I loved it, it was a hell of a book. And then I spoke to Harry Cohn, who was then the head of Columbia Pictures and a friend. And I said, 'I'd like to play that.' He said, 'Well, you've never done a dramatic role. You're a guy who sings and dances with Gene Kelly.'"

at its very best, richer than it had been, more knowing. And here came a bandleader with new ideas and shadings. Frank and Nelse could swing like nobody's business, then take you to the wee small hours. You'd had a tough day, so you mixed yourself a Flame of Love Martini, the kind Pepe Ruiz made for the fellows at Chasen's. And Sinatra took you along—to April in Paris, to autumn in New York. To Vegas. To the moon. To wherever the Chairman wanted to go. Late at night, you danced in the dark.

Guys Sinatra's age started to wear hats the way he wore his hat. Sinatra declared orange—*orange!*—"the national color," so all of a sudden there was a run on orange sweaters. In the late '50s, early '60s, America was buzzing with high hopes, and everybody felt very . . . ring-a-ding. Did Sinatra reflect it or invent it? "He created eras," said Tony Bennett, who was there. "He made us think his way."

Times had changed, and the things that Sinatra had once been savaged for—the nightclubbing, the photogbashing, the chick-chasing—now earned him style points. He was absolutely bulletproof.

And, man, did he act like it.

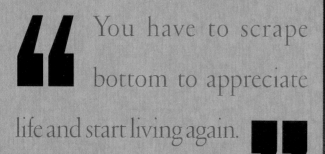

"You have to scrape bottom to appreciate life and start living again."

From Here to Eternity was released in August '53, but Sinatra knew he had a shot even before then. On April 30, he'd been introduced to 32-year-old Nelson Riddle, who had arrangements for "I've Got the World on a String" and "Don't Worry 'Bout Me." Sinatra cut the tunes, heard the playback and declared, **"I'm back."** In 1954 the partnership's "Young at Heart" went to No. 2, Sinatra's first hit in seven years.

PHIL STERN/CPI

Everyone could hear the change in Sinatra's singing (below). His son said that soon after Riddle came on the scene, "Pop was putting more energy into it, belting a little more. His whole attitude was becoming **a little more hip now.** The curly-haired, bow-tied image was gone. Now there was the long tie—and the hat, that Cavanaugh hat."

"Gasoline" was always at hand—usually *in* hand—whether Sinatra was making a movie (Burt Lancaster remembered carrying him to bed every night during the filming of *Eternity*) or harmonizing with Nat "King" Cole (right). In early 1954, Sinatra enlisted in Humphrey Bogart's L.A.-based "Rat Pack." Said Bogie's wife, Lauren Bacall: "In order to qualify, one had to be **addicted to nonconformity,** staying up late, drinking, laughing and not caring what anyone thought or said about us."

> " Luck is fine, and you have to have luck to get the opportunity. But after that, you've got to have talent and know how to use it. "

In 1954 Sinatra played the role of Nathan Detroit in the film version of *Guys and Dolls* (left). He had **wanted the romantic lead,** Sky Masterson, which went to Marlon Brando. But Sinatra left nothing unfinished: Years later, when he made an album of the score, he sang the Masterson part.

If Sinatra was at a lunch on the *G&D* set (above), Brando was usually absent. **The two despised each other.** "The most overrated actor in the world," said Sinatra. Brando rejoined: "When he dies and goes to heaven, the first thing he'll do will be to find God and yell at him for making him bald."

65

After being jilted by Gardner, Sinatra hooked up with Lauren Bacall, whom he jilted in 1958. ("My humiliation was indescribable," she said.) He then went on the prowl until his liaison with dancer Juliet Prowse (left) led to **a betrothal of sorts.** Was the February 1962 engagement, announced by Sinatra himself—"I'm 46 now. It's time I settled down"—the real thing? Or was it a publicity stunt to boost his young amour's career? Whatever, it was over in an eye-blink, ostensibly because she refused to quit working. "Talk about short engagements," quipped Johnny Carson, "Frank has had longer engagements in Las Vegas."

BOB WILLOUGHBY

"I love being a father and a grandfather," he said. "I love having the house full." But as a family man, his track record was uneven. He divorced his children's mother and in pursuit of his career was often away. "I have been at times lax, very lax, in my duties as a father," he admitted to Nancy Jr. in a 1985 TV interview. But he loved his children deeply and would do for them what he could, when he could—as here, in 1955, when he visited Nancy's Los Angeles high school to sing a duet with his daughter. In the **tender moments** seen here: He straightens her collar, opposite, and tries to calm her nerves, top. The day a grand success, he drives off as her classmates squeal. Nancy Sr. kept Frank involved as an absentee father. She'd call him when one of the children misbehaved, and he'd do the grounding over the phone. He lavished gifts on his children, especially his daughters, and never raised a hand to them. (He dressed down his friend Bing Crosby over what he considered Crosby's tyrannical treatment of his sons.) There were undeniable advantages to being Frank Sinatra's child, as Tina learned when Dad called Soupy Sales and said, "I'm Frank Sinatra. My kid wants me to do your show." There were disadvantages, too. One day, Tina complained about all the people staring at her. "They're not staring at you, Pigeon," her father said sympathetically. "They're staring at me." As Frank's son, Frankie had it toughest. The most difficult time for the family came on December 8, 1963, when Frank Jr. was kidnapped at Lake Tahoe. "I'd give the world for my son," said an anguished Sinatra, who paid a $240,000 ransom. Later, the defense team for the kidnappers claimed it had all been a publicity stunt staged by the Sinatras. (Said Frank, "This family needs publicity like it needs peritonitis.") Frankie bounced back from the trauma; later in life, he would lead his dad's orchestra. Nancy Jr. would become her dad's Boswell, not only writing biographies but creating a Sinatra family Web site. Tina would produce a critically acclaimed TV miniseries about her dad. The Sinatra kids would thrive, and Frank would give credit where it was due: "Nancy did one hell of a job raising our kids."

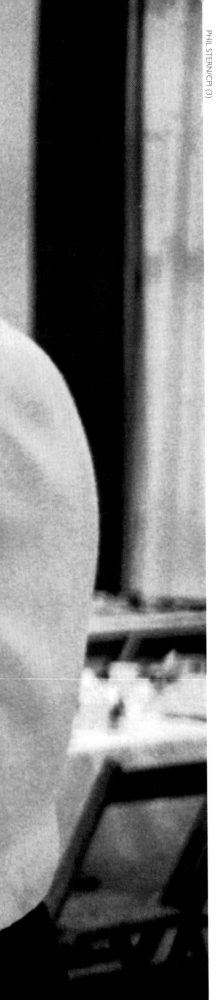

In 1960 Sinatra marshaled the Hollywood troops on behalf of John F. Kennedy. The campaign's theme, **"High Hopes,"** was based on the effervescent Sinatra-Riddle collaboration. (Sinatra had lyricist Sammy Cahn customize a pro-Kennedy verse.) Once the votes were in, Sinatra set to work orchestrating the inaugural gala. He recruited friends Gene Kelly and Peter Lawford (top), greeted Ella Fitzgerald (left) and rehearsed with Lawford, Tony Curtis, Nat Cole and Janet Leigh (above). Ella was always Sinatra's favorite. When he embarked on his big-selling but artistically wanting *Duets* projects in the 1990s, his first question was "How is Ella doing?" She wasn't doing well enough to be coaxed into the studio, and so the two greatest interpreters of American song never did record together. They harmonized, however, on three TV specials; the 1967 *A Man and His Music + Ella + Jobim* was true magic.

Scenes circa 1960: Lawford, Sinatra and Marilyn Monroe—all close to JFK in different ways, as we now know—schmoozed in Santa Monica, Calif. (below), while on a fancier occasion, the new President accepted a light from the man who had been instrumental in getting him elected. It wasn't just Sinatra's singing that had aided the cause, it was his connections. Early on, when Joseph P. Kennedy asked Sinatra for help in the crucial West Virginia primary—could Frank talk to his friend Sam Giancana?—the singer went to the mobster, the mobster went to the coal miners' union, and JFK went on to the nomination. Giancana was also at the heart of the split between Sinatra and the President.

In 1962, Bobby Kennedy told his brother to **steer clear of the mob-linked singer.** Sinatra, meanwhile, had just finished the "Kennedy Wing" of his Palm Springs compound, dreaming it would be the Hyannis Port of the desert. When JFK changed his plan to stay at Sinatra's, opting for Bing Crosby's house up the road, Sinatra was infuriated. The rift looked permanent. Was it? "For a brief moment, he was the brightest star in our lives," Sinatra said much later. "I loved him." On the door of his guest room, he kept a polished plaque: JOHN F. KENNEDY SLEPT HERE, NOVEMBER 6TH AND 7TH 1960.

Humphrey Bogart's Rat Pack sat around his L.A. home, giving out titles: Judy Garland was first veep, agent Swifty Lazar was secretary, writer Nathaniel Benchley was historian, the new kid Sinatra was "pack master." Said Bogie: "We admire ourselves and don't care for anyone else."

After the actor died in 1957, Sinatra, who had idolized him, relocated and recast the Rat Pack while maintaining its credo. The core members of **Sinatra's Pack,** seen opposite and above, included Dean Martin, Sammy Davis Jr., Peter Lawford and Joey Bishop. Orbiting were Shirley MacLaine (seen as "the mascot" by Pack Rats), Tony Curtis, Garland, a gang of others. They would come and go, not at their whim but at Sinatra's. After JFK didn't show up in Palm Springs, Lawford, who had earlier been temporarily banished for dating Ava Gardner, was out for good: As a Kennedy in-law, he was persona non grata. Lawford was booted not only from the next Rat Pack movie (4 for Texas) but, 20 years later, from his table at the Sands; Sinatra wouldn't go on until Lawford was gonesville. Even Sammy could be exiled: The poor guy had said to a journalist, "I don't care if you are the most talented person in the world. It doesn't give you the right to step on people and treat them rotten." Sammy was forced to issue a public

apology before being allowed back into the Pack.

Why did they all take it? Because one Rat Pack rule read, "The King can do no wrong." And because, inside the Pack, it was a hell of a lot of fun. Dean Martin said, "When it was bad between you and Frank, it was piss-poor bad," but added, "When it was good, it was so good, you had to be there."

"There" was a nightspot, with a woman and a drink convenient. As far as the drinking went, it wasn't as bad as all that—it was worse. Consider: Dino's storied love of the sauce was matched by his mates'. "I spill more than he drinks," said Sinatra, "and that's an actuality." The cart they pushed onstage at the Sands bore the motto DON'T THIMK, DRIMK. Challenged by his doctor, Sinatra admitted to **three dozen drinks a day.** The doctor, horrified, asked how he felt each morning. "I don't know," said Sinatra. "I'm never up in the morning. And I'm not sure you're the doctor for me."

The Rat Pack

Frank Sinatra (Leader)
Dean Martin
Sammy Davis Jr.
Peter Lawford
Joey Bishop
Shirley MacLaine (Mascot)

Pack Associates

Tony Curtis
Janet Leigh
Judy Garland
Brad Dexter
Joe E. Lewis
Sammy Cahn
Jimmy Van Heusen
Steve Lawrence
Kirk Douglas
Don Rickles
Robert Wagner
Richard Conte
George Raft
Eddie Fisher

Rat Pack Lingo

broad (n.): a sexy woman

charlies (n.): sexy breasts

chick (n.): a young sexy woman

clyde (n.): means anything

crazy (adj.): cool

crumb (n.): a creep

gasoline (n.): booze

gasser (n.): a great person

harve (n.): a square

mouse (n.): a small woman

player (n.): a gambler with brio

ring-a-ding (adj.): terrific

twirl (n.): a chick who loves dancing

–ville (suffix): many uses; *bombsville, endsville, splitsville*

The year was 1965. As the months marched on to December, Sinatra was cruising toward 50 years of age. The world would pay proper attention; television would salute the anniversary, as would the tabloids, which still loved and loathed the guy.

"Frank Sinatra at 50" seemed a perfect story for *Esquire* magazine, and *Esquire*'s celebrated Gay Talese seemed—and was—the perfect writer for the job. Talese traveled to L.A. that autumn to catch up with Sinatra, but Frank wasn't felling well, and therefore he wasn't in the mood. So, of course, things weren't happening.

Or were they? Talese, the quintessential journalist, observed and began to make notes. He came to conclusions about the dynamics of the Sinatra scene, about what made the man tick, about what fueled the swirl around him (besides the alcohol). He knew the background thoroughly and brought the background to bear on the present reality, or surreality. And then he sat down and started to paint his pictures.

Talese was and is a . . .

Well, he's a Sinatra of scriveners—not a practitioner, but an artist. And in the early and mid-1960s he was more than a stylist, more, even, than a pro. He was a revolutionary. There was something afoot at the time, a movement that would come to be called the New Journalism, which all these years later remains a complicated and ill-defined concept but which, in short, saw the craftsperson employing techniques of fiction writing as well as first-person observation in creating a narrative or portrait through scenes and settings. Truman Capote, Joan Didion, Tom Wolfe and others were pioneering a radically different, engrossing kind of nonfiction, and Talese was at the head. Many critics have opined that "Frank Sinatra Has a Cold" can make a claim as *the* seminal work of New Journalism, the piece that proved the possibilities. Whatever, it is a masterwork. With seamless technique that fascinates and almost befuddles—*how is he doing this?*—Talese told us who Sinatra was and why. When *Esquire* magazine, celebrating its own 70th birthday in 2003, chose the best article to ever appear in its pages, it anointed this one.

Back in 1965, "Frank Sinatra at 50" seemed a perfect topic for LIFE magazine, too, and as LIFE was known for telling stories through pictures, it looked to its roster of photojournalists and picked the esteemed John Dominis—a Talese (or a Sinatra) among shutterbugs. Dominis went west as Talese did and hovered in the shadows as Talese did. For a photo essay, of course, he needed access. He didn't shoot a frame for days but did gain the trust and confidence of Sinatra, who was an enthusiastic amateur photographer himself. Eventually, Dominis was invited in. Over four months he shot some 4,000 images; he was everywhere—Vegas, Palm Springs, New York, Miami—he was part of the Pack. "Back then," he reminisces today, "I was young enough to enjoy all the wild parties. I'll tell you, I had fun."

Ever since we at LIFE Books first issued *Remembering Sinatra* 10 years ago, it has been in the back of our collective mind what a perfect pairing—like Scotch and soda—the twin documents of Talese and Dominis might make. With the gracious permission of both artists, this now comes to pass.

And so here, from the swingin' '60s:

FRANK SINATRA HAS A COLD

FRANK SINATRA, HOLDING A GLASS OF BOURBON IN one hand and a cigarette in the other, stood in a dark corner of the bar between two attractive but fading blondes who sat waiting for him to say something. But he said nothing; he had been silent

during much of the evening, except now in this private club in Beverly Hills he seemed even more distant, staring out through the smoke and semidarkness into a large room beyond the bar where dozens of young couples sat huddled around small tables or twisted in the center of the floor to the clamorous clang of folk-rock music blaring from the stereo. The two blondes knew, as did Sinatra's four male friends who stood nearby, that it was a bad idea to force conversation upon him when he was in this mood of sullen silence, a mood that had hardly been uncommon during this first week of November, a month before his fiftieth birthday.

Sinatra had been working in a film that he now disliked, could not wait to finish; he was tired of all the publicity attached to his dating the twenty-year-old Mia Farrow, who was not in sight tonight; he was angry that a CBS television documentary of his life, to be shown in two weeks, was reportedly prying into his privacy, even speculating on his possible friendship with Mafia leaders; he was worried about his starring role in an hour-long NBC show entitled *Sinatra—A Man and His Music*, which would require that he sing eighteen songs with a voice that at this particular moment, just a few nights before the taping was to begin, was weak and sore and uncertain. Sinatra was ill. He was the victim of an ailment so common that most people would consider it trivial. But when it gets to Sinatra it can plunge him into a state of anguish, deep depression, panic, even rage. Frank Sinatra had a cold.

BY GAY TALESE
PHOTOGRAPHS BY JOHN DOMINIS

Sinatra with a cold is Picasso without paint, Ferrari without fuel—only worse. For the common cold robs Sinatra of that uninsurable jewel, his voice, cutting into the core of his confidence, and it affects not only his own psyche but also seems to cause a kind of psychosomatic nasal drip within dozens of people who work for him, drink with him, love him, depend on him for their own welfare and stability. A Sinatra with a cold can, in a small way, send vibrations through the entertainment industry and beyond as surely as a President of the United States, suddenly sick, can shake the national economy.

For Frank Sinatra was now involved with many things involving many people—his own film company, his record company, his private airline, his missile-parts firm, his real-estate holdings across the nation, his personal staff of seventy-five—which are only a portion of the power he is and has come to represent. He seemed now to be also the embodiment of the fully emancipated male, perhaps the only one in America, the man who can do anything he wants, anything, can do it because he has money, the energy, and no apparent guilt. In an age when the very young seem to be taking over, protesting and picketing and demanding change, Frank Sinatra survives as a national phenomenon, one of the few prewar products to withstand the test of time. He is the champ who made the big comeback, the man who had everything, lost it, then got it back, letting nothing stand in his way, doing what few men can do: he uprooted his life, left his family, broke with everything that was familiar, learning in the process that one way to hold a woman is not to hold her. Now he has the affection of Nancy and Ava and Mia, the fine female produce of three generations, and still has the adoration of his children, the freedom of a bachelor, he does not feel old, he makes old men feel young, makes them think that if Frank Sinatra can do it, it can be done; not that they could do it, but it is still nice for other men to know, at fifty, that it can be done.

But now, standing at this bar in Beverly Hills, Sinatra had a cold, and he continued to drink quietly and he seemed miles away in his private world, not even reacting when suddenly the stereo in the other room switched to a Sinatra song, "In the Wee Small Hours of the Morning."

It is a lovely ballad that he first recorded ten years ago, and it now inspired many young couples who had been sitting, tired of twisting, to get up and move slowly around the dance floor, holding one another very close. Sinatra's intonation, precisely clipped, yet full and flowing, gave a deeper meaning to the simple lyrics—"In the wee small hours of the morning/while the whole wide world is fast asleep/you lie awake, and think about the girl…."—it was like so many of his classics, a song that evoked loneliness and sensuality, and when blended with the dim light and the alcohol and nicotine and late-night needs, it became a kind of airy aphrodisiac. Undoubtedly the words from this song, and others like it, had put millions in the mood, it was music to make love by, and doubtless much love had been made by it all over America at night in cars, while the batteries burned down, in cottages by the lake, on beaches during balmy summer evenings, in secluded parks and exclusive penthouses and furnished rooms, in cabin cruisers and cabs and cabanas—in all places where Sinatra's songs could be heard were these words that warmed women, wooed and won them, snipped the final thread of inhibition and gratified the male egos of ungrateful lovers; two generations of men had been the beneficiaries of such ballads, for which they were eternally in his debt, for which they may eternally hate him. Nevertheless here he was, the man himself, in the early hours of the morning in Beverly Hills, out of range.

The two blondes, who seemed to be in their middle thirties, were preened and polished, their matured bodies softly molded within tight dark suits. They sat, legs crossed, perched on the high bar stools. They listened to the music. Then one of them pulled out a Kent and Sinatra quickly placed his gold lighter under it and she held his hand, looked at his fingers: they were nubby and raw, and the pinkies protruded, being so stiff from arthritis that he could barely bend them. He was, as usual, immaculately dressed. He wore an oxford-grey suit with a vest, a suit conservatively cut on the outside but trimmed with flamboyant silk within; his shoes, British, seemed to be shined even on the bottom of the soles. He also wore, as

Considering his profession, Sinatra's lifestyle was counterproductive in the long and, sometimes, short term. The booze was a problem, so were the cigarettes—and Sinatra knew it. Once, when his voice just wasn't there and he had to sing on a television show, he was in the corner muttering, "Drink, drink, drink. Smoke, smoke, smoke. **Schmuck, schmuck, schmuck."** But later that night—very safe bet—he had a drink or six and inhaled his share. For he also said, many a time, "You die your way. I'll die mine."

everybody seemed to know, a remarkably convincing black hairpiece, one of sixty that he owns, most of them under the care of an inconspicuous little grey-haired lady who, holding his hair in a tiny satchel, follows him around whenever he performs. She earns $400 a week. The most distinguishing thing about Sinatra's face are his eyes, clear blue and alert, eyes that within seconds can go cold with anger, or glow with affection, or, as now, reflect a vague detachment that keeps his friends silent and distant.

Leo Durocher, one of Sinatra's closest friends, was now shooting pool in the small room behind the bar. Standing near the door was Jim Mahoney, Sinatra's press agent, a somewhat chunky young man with a square jaw and narrow eyes who would resemble a tough Irish plainclothesman if it were not for the expensive continental suits he wears and his exquisite shoes often adorned with polished buckles. Also nearby was a big, broad-shouldered two-hundred-pound actor named Brad Dexter who seemed always to be thrusting out his chest so that his gut would not show.

Brad Dexter has appeared in several films and television shows, displaying fine talent as a character actor, but in Beverly Hills he is equally known for the role he played in Hawaii two years ago when he swam a few hundred yards and risked his life to save Sinatra from drowning in a riptide. Since then Dexter has been one of Sinatra's constant companions and has been made a producer in Sinatra's film company. He occupies a plush office near Sinatra's executive suite. He is endlessly searching for literary properties that might be converted into new starring roles for Sinatra. Whenever he is among strangers with Sinatra he worries because he knows that Sinatra brings out the best and worst in people—some men will become aggressive, some women will become seductive, others will stand around skeptically appraising him, the scene will be somehow intoxicated by his mere presence, and maybe Sinatra himself, if feeling as badly as he was tonight, might become intolerant or tense, and then: headlines. So Brad Dexter tries to anticipate danger and warn Sinatra in advance. He confesses to feeling very protective of Sinatra, admitting

The LIFE article that ran with John Dominis's photo essay had this to say about the scene at right: "It was six a.m. before the party got to Frank's suite. But the evening was not over because **Frank hadn't said it was over.** 'Everybody have a little more gasoline,' he ordered. Everybody did. They threw darts at a target on the wall. Frank was good at it. From the kitchen came a shout. A couple of guys were wrestling around. Frank went to see. Somebody got a raw egg broken on him. Then somebody else did. The sun was up at seven when Frank announced he was going to bed." And so was Jilly Rizzo (left) and bodyguard Ed Pucci (in front of the fridge). And so were a dozen other stragglers, all going to bed. For when Frank said the party was over, it was over.

in a recent moment of self-revelation: "I'd kill for him."

While this statement may seem outlandishly dramatic, particularly when taken out of context, it nonetheless expresses a fierce fidelity that is quite common within Sinatra's special circle. It is a characteristic that Sinatra, without admission, seems to prefer: All the Way; All or Nothing at All. This is the Sicilian in Sinatra; he permits his friends, if they wish to remain that, none of the easy Anglo-Saxon outs. But if they remain loyal, then there is nothing

Sinatra will not do in turn—fabulous gifts, personal kindnesses, encouragement when they're down, adulation when they're up. They are wise to remember, however, one thing. He is Sinatra. The boss. *Il Padrone.*

I had seen something of this Sicilian side of Sinatra last summer at Jilly's saloon in New York, which was the only other time I'd gotten a close view of him prior to this night in this California club. Jilly's, which is on West Fifty-second Street in Manhattan, is where Sinatra drinks whenever he is in New York, and there is a special chair reserved for him in the back room against the wall that nobody else may use. When he is occupying it, seated behind a long table flanked by his closest New York friends—who include the saloonkeeper, Jilly Rizzo, and Jilly's azure-haired wife, Honey, who is known as the "Blue Jew"—a rather strange ritualistic scene develops. That night dozens of people, some of them casual friends of Sinatra's, some mere acquaintances, some neither, appeared outside of Jilly's saloon. They

approached it like a shrine. They had come to pay respect. They were from New York, Brooklyn, Atlantic City, Hoboken. They were old actors, young actors, former prize-fighters, tired trumpet players, politicians, a boy with a cane. There was a fat lady who said she remembered Sinatra when he used to throw the *Jersey Observer* onto her front porch in 1933. There were middle-aged couples who said they had heard Sinatra sing at the Rustic Cabin in 1938 and "We knew then that he really had it!" Or they had heard him when he was with Harry James's band in 1939, or with Tommy Dorsey in 1941 ("Yeah, that's the song, 'I'll Never Smile Again'—he sang it one night in this dump near Newark and we danced . . ."); or they remembered that time at the Paramount with the swooners, and him with those bow ties, The Voice; and one woman remembered that awful boy she knew then—Alexander Dorogokupetz, an eighteen-year-old heckler who had thrown a tomato at Sinatra and the bobby-soxers in the balcony had tried to flail him to death. Whatever became of Alexander Dorogokupetz? The lady did not know.

And they remembered when Sinatra was a failure and sang trash like "Mairzy Doats," and they remembered his comeback and on this night they were all standing outside Jilly's saloon, dozens of them, but they could not get in. So some of them left. But most of them stayed, hoping that soon they might be able to push or wedge their way into Jilly's between the elbows and backsides of the men drinking three-deep at the bar, and they might be able to peek through and see him sitting back there. This is all they really wanted; they wanted to see him. And for a few moments they gazed in silence through the smoke and they stared. Then they turned, fought their way out of the bar, went home.

Some of Sinatra's close friends, all of whom are known to the men guarding Jilly's door, do manage to get an escort into the back room. But once they are there they, too, must fend for themselves. On the particular evening, Frank Gifford, the

At **a party in Miami,** Sinatra told Ed Pucci he could pull off the tablecloth without disturbing the china. For Sinatra, it was a good thing gambling was against the law in Florida (not, of course, that this would have prevented his wager).

former football player, got only seven yards in three tries. Others who had somehow been close enough to shake Sinatra's hand did not shake it; instead they just touched him on the shoulder or sleeve, or they merely stood close enough for him to see them and, after he'd given them a wink of recognition or a wave or a nod or called out their names (he had a fantastic memory for first names), they would then turn and leave. They had checked in. They had paid their respects. And as I watched this ritualistic scene, I got the impression that Frank Sinatra was dwelling simultaneously in two worlds that were not contemporary.

On the one hand he is the swinger—as he is when talking and joking with Sammy Davis, Jr., Richard Conte, Liza Minelli, Bernie Massi, or any of the other show-business people who get to sit at the table; on the other, as when he is nodding or waving to his paisanos who are close to him (Al Silvani, a boxing manager who works with Sinatra's film company; Dominic Di Bona, his wardrobe man; Ed Pucci, a three-hundred-pound former football lineman who is his aide-de-camp), Frank Sinatra is *Il Padrone*. Or better still, he is what in traditional Sicily have long been called *uomini rispettati*—men of respect: men who are both majestic and humble, men who are loved by all and are very generous by nature, men whose hands are kissed as they walk from village to village, men who would personally go out of their way to redress a wrong.

Frank Sinatra does things personally. At Christmas time, he will personally pick dozens of presents for his close friends and family, remembering the type of jewelry they like, their favorite colors, the sizes of their shirts and dresses. When a musician friend's house was destroyed and his wife was killed in a Los Angeles mud slide a little more than a year ago, Sinatra personally came to his aid, finding the musician a new home, paying whatever hospital bills

were left unpaid by the insurance, then personally supervising the furnishing of the new home down to the replacing of the silverware, the linen, the purchase of new clothing.

The same Sinatra who did this can, within the same hour, explode in a towering rage of intolerance should a small thing be incorrectly done for him by one of his paisanos. For example, when one of his men brought him a frankfurter with catsup on it, which Sinatra apparently abhors, he angrily threw the bottle at the man, splattering catsup all over him. Most of the men who work around Sinatra are big. But this never seems to intimidate Sinatra nor curb his impetuous behavior with them when he is mad. They will never take a swing back at him. He is *Il Padrone*.

At other times, aiming to please, his men will overreact to his desires: when he casually observed that his big orange desert jeep in Palm Springs seemed in need of a new painting, the word was swiftly passed down through the channels, becoming ever more urgent as it went, until finally it was a command that the jeep be painted now, immediately, yesterday. To accomplish this would require the hiring of a special crew of painters to work all night, at overtime rates; which, in turn, meant that the order had to be bucked back up the line for further approval. When it finally got back to Sinatra's desk, he did not know what it was all about; after he had figured it out he confessed, with a tired look on his face, that he did not care when the hell they painted the jeep.

Yet it would have been unwise for anyone to anticipate his reaction, for he is a wholly unpredictable man of many moods and great dimension, a man who responds instantaneously to instinct—suddenly, dramatically, wildly he responds, and nobody can predict what will follow. A young lady named Jane Hoag, a reporter at LIFE's Los Angeles bureau who had attended the same school as Sinatra's daughter, Nancy, had once been invited to a party at Mrs. Sinatra's California home at which Frank Sinatra, who maintains very cordial relations with his former wife, acted as host. Early in the party Miss Hoag, while leaning against a table, accidentally with her elbow knocked over one of a pair of alabaster birds to the floor, smashing it to pieces.

Suddenly, Miss Hoag recalled, Sinatra's daughter cried, "Oh, that was one of my mother's favorite . . ."—but before she could complete the sentence, Sinatra glared at her, cutting her off, and while forty other guests in the room all stared

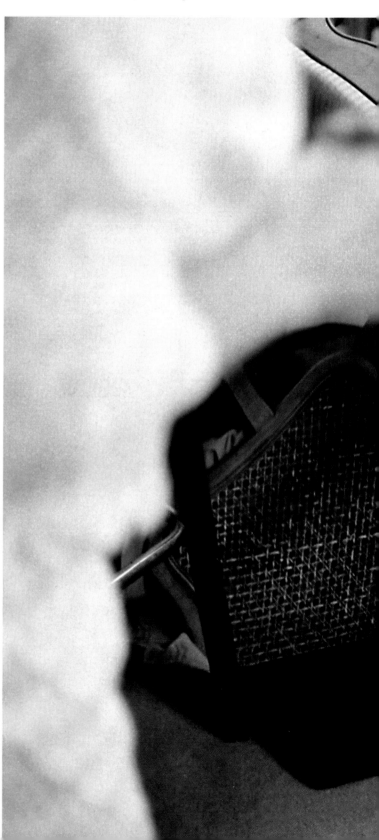

in silence, Sinatra walked over, quickly with his finger flicked the other alabaster bird off the table, smashing it to pieces, and then put an arm gently around Jane Hoag and said, in a way that put her completely at ease, "That's okay, kid."

N OW SINATRA SAID A FEW WORDS TO THE blondes. Then he turned from the bar and began to walk toward the poolroom. One of Sinatra's other men friends moved in to keep the girls company. Brad

A select few comics really slayed Sinatra. Joey Bishop could always bust him up, as could Pack associate Joe E. Lewis. "This was also in Miami," remembers photographer Dominis. "Sinatra and Lewis were appearing there for two weeks. Sinatra invited me to the party—he said the people at the party were okay to be photographed, it wasn't a bunch of Mafia characters. He was **fooling around all night** with Lewis, singing and so forth. When Lewis told this one joke, Sinatra fell right off his chair." Maybe the line had been that old Lewis staple, oft-quoted by Sinatra, not always with attribution: "You're not drunk if you can lie on the floor without holding on."

Dexter, who had been standing in the corner talking to some other people, now followed Sinatra.

The room cracked with the clack of billiard balls. There were about a dozen spectators in the room, most of them young men who were watching Leo Durocher shoot against two other aspiring hustlers who were not very good. This private drinking club has among its membership many actors, directors, writers, models, nearly all of them a good deal younger than Sinatra or Durocher and much more casual in the way they dress for the evening. Many of the young women, their long hair flowing loosely below their shoulders, wore tight, fanny-fitting Jax pants and very expensive sweaters; and a few of the young men wore blue or green velour shirts with high collars and narrow tight pants, and Italian loafers.

It was obvious from the way Sinatra looked at these people in the poolroom that they were not his style, but he leaned back against a high stool that was against the wall, holding his drink in his right hand, and said nothing, just watched Durocher slam the billiard balls back and forth. The younger men in the room, accustomed to seeing Sinatra at this club, treated him without deference, although they said nothing offensive. They were a cool young group, very California-cool and casual, and one of the coolest seemed to be a little guy, very quick of movement, who had a sharp profile, pale blue eyes, blondish hair, and squared eyeglasses. He wore a pair of brown corduroy slacks, a green shaggy-dog Shetland sweater, a tan suede jacket, and Game Warden boots, for which he had recently paid $60.

Frank Sinatra, leaning against the stool, sniffling a bit from his cold, could not take his eyes off the Game Warden boots. Once, after gazing at

them for a few moments, he turned away; but now he was focused on them again. The owner of the boots, who was just standing in them watching the pool game, was named Harlan Ellison, a writer who had just completed work on a screenplay, *The Oscar*.

Finally Sinatra could not contain himself.

"Hey," he yelled in his slightly harsh voice that still had a soft, sharp edge. "Those Italian boots?"

"No," Ellison said.

"Spanish?"

"No."

"Are they English boots?"

"Look, I donno, man," Ellison shot back, frowning at Sinatra, then turning away again.

Now the poolroom was suddenly silent. Leo Durocher who had been poised behind his cue stick and was bent low just froze in that position for a second. Nobody moved. Then Sinatra moved away from the stool and walked with that slow, arrogant swagger of his toward Ellison, the hard tap of Sinatra's shoes the only sound in the room. Then, looking down at Ellison with a slightly raised eyebrow and a tricky little smile, Sinatra asked: "You expecting a storm?"

Harlan Ellison moved a step to the side. "Look, is there any reason why you're talking to me?"

"I don't like the way you're dressed," Sinatra said.

"Hate to shake you up," Ellison said, "but I dress to suit myself."

Now there was some rumbling in the room, and somebody said, "Com'on, Harlan, let's get out of here," and Leo Durocher made his pool shot and said, "Yeah, com'on."

But Ellison stood his ground.

Sinatra said, "What do you do?"

"I'm a plumber," Ellison said.

"No, no, he's not," another young man quickly yelled from across the table. "He wrote *The Oscar.*"

"Oh, yeah," Sinatra said, "well I've seen it, and it's a piece of crap."

"That's strange," Ellison said, "because they haven't even released it yet."

"Well, I've seen it," Sinatra repeated, "and it's a piece of crap."

Now Brad Dexter, very anxious, very big opposite the small figure of Ellison, said, "Com'on, kid, I don't want you in this room."

"Hey," Sinatra interrupted Dexter, "can't you see I'm talking to this guy?"

Dexter was confused. Then his whole attitude changed, and his voice went soft and he said to Ellison, almost with a plea, "Why do you persist in tormenting me?"

The whole scene was becoming ridiculous, and it seemed that Sinatra was only half-serious, perhaps just reacting out of sheer boredom or inner despair; at any rate, after a few more exchanges Harlan Ellison left the room. By this time the word had gotten out to those on the dance floor about the Sinatra-Ellison exchange, and somebody went to look for the manager of the club. But somebody else said that the manager had already heard about

Frank got smooched by Dino and caressed by Sammy. To **the color-blind Sinatra,** Davis was as much a paisano as Martin. When Davis caused a scandal by wedding the Swede Mai Britt in 1960, Sinatra was best man. "For him to state, 'This is my friend, and you can stick it in your ear' meant putting in jeopardy everything he's worked for," said Sammy. "It was not a minor thing."

it—and had quickly gone out the door, hopped in his car and drove home. So the assistant manager went into the poolroom.

"I don't want anybody in here without coats and ties," Sinatra snapped.

The assistant manager nodded, and walked back to his office.

IT WAS THE MORNING AFTER. IT WAS THE beginning of another nervous day for Sinatra's press agent, Jim Mahoney. Mahoney had a headache, and he was worried but not over the Sinatra-Ellison incident of the night before. At the time Mahoney had been with his wife at a table in the other room, and possibly he had not even been aware of the little drama. The whole thing had lasted only about three minutes. And three minutes after it was over, Frank Sinatra had probably forgotten about it for the rest of his life— as Ellison will probably remember it for the rest of his life: he had had, as hundreds of others before him, at an unexpected moment between darkness and dawn, a scene with Sinatra.

It was just as well that Mahoney had not been in the poolroom; he had enough on his mind today. He was worried about Sinatra's cold and worried about the controversial CBS documentary that, despite Sinatra's protests and withdrawal of permission, would be shown on television in

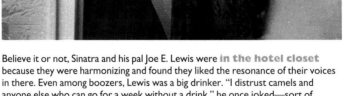

Believe it or not, Sinatra and his pal Joe E. Lewis were **in the hotel closet** because they were harmonizing and found they liked the resonance of their voices in there. Even among boozers, Lewis was a big drinker. "I distrust camels and anyone else who can go for a week without a drink," he once joked—sort of.

less than two weeks. The newspapers this morning were full of hints that Sinatra might sue the network, and Mahoney's phones were ringing without pause, and now he was plugged into New York talking to the *Daily News*'s Kay Gardella, saying:" …that's right, Kay …they made a gentleman's agreement to not ask certain questions about Frank's private life, and then Cronkite went right ahead:'Frank, tell me about those associations.' That question, Kay—out! That question should never have been asked…."

As he spoke, Mahoney leaned back in his leather chair, his head shaking slowly. He is a powerfully built man of thirty-seven; he has a round, ruddy face, a heavy jaw, and narrow pale eyes, and he might appear pugnacious if he did not speak with such clear, soft sincerity and if he were not so meticulous about his clothes. His suits and shoes are superbly tailored, which was one of the first things Sinatra noticed about him, and in his spacious office opposite the bar is a red-muff electrical shoe polisher and a pair of brown wooden shoulders on a stand over which Mahoney can drape his jackets. Near the bar is an autographed photograph of President Kennedy and a few pictures of Frank Sinatra, but there are none of Sinatra in any other rooms in Mahoney's public-relations agency; there once was a large photograph of him hanging in the reception room but this apparently bruised the egos of some of Mahoney's other movie-star clients and, since Sinatra never shows up at the agency anyway, the photograph was removed.

Still, Sinatra seems ever present, and if Mahoney did not have legitimate worries about Sinatra, as he did today, he could invent them—and, as worry aids, he surrounds himself with little mementos of moments in the past when he did worry. In his shaving kit there is a two-year-old box of sleeping tablets dispensed by a Reno druggist—the date on the bottle marks the kidnapping of Frank Sinatra, Jr. There is on a table in Mahoney's office a mounted wood reproduction of Frank Sinatra's ransom note written on the aforementioned occasion. One of Mahoney's mannerisms, when he is sitting at his desk worrying, is to tinker with the tiny toy train he keeps in front of him—the train is a souvenir from the Sinatra film, *Von Ryan's Express;* it is to men who are close to Sinatra what the PT-109 tie clasps are to men who were close to Kennedy—and Mahoney then proceeds to roll the little train back and forth on the six inches of track; back and forth, back and forth, *click-clack-click-clack.* It is his Queeg-thing.

Now Mahoney quickly put aside the little train. His secretary told him there was a very important call on the line. Mahoney picked it up, and his voice was even softer and more sincere than before. "Yes, Frank," he said. "Right ... right ... yes, Frank...."

When Mahoney put down the phone, quietly, he announced that Frank Sinatra had left in his private jet to spend the weekend at his home in Palm Springs, which is a

Sinatra lit a cigarette for the actress Natalie Wood. He could be **extremely kind,** and he could be just as cruel—with women as well as men. Like most of Sinatra's love affairs, the one with Wood was stormy; he once berated her so mercilessly at a party in his home that she fled in tears.

sixteen-minute flight from his home in Los Angeles. Mahoney was now worried again. The Lear jet that Sinatra's pilot would be flying was identical, Mahoney said, to the one that had just crashed in another part of California.

ON THE FOLLOWING MONDAY, A CLOUDY and unseasonably cool California day, more than one hundred people gathered inside a white television studio, an enormous room dominated by a white stage, white walls, and with dozens of lights and lamps dangling: it rather resembled a gigantic operating room. In this room, within an hour or so, NBC was scheduled to begin taping a one-hour show that would be televised in color on the night of November 24 and would highlight, as much as it could in the limited time, the twenty-five-year career of Frank Sinatra as a public entertainer. It would not attempt to probe, as the forthcoming CBS Sinatra documentary allegedly would, that area of Sinatra's life that he regards as private. The NBC show would be mainly an hour of Sinatra singing some of the hits that carried him from Hoboken to Hollywood, a show that would be interrupted only now and then by a few film clips and commercials for Budweiser beer. Prior to his cold, Sinatra had been very excited about this show; he saw here an opportunity to appeal not only to those nostalgic, but also to communicate his talent to some rock-and-rollers—in a sense, he was battling The Beatles. The press releases being prepared by Mahoney's agency stressed this, reading: "If you happen to be tired of kid singers wearing mops of hair thick enough to hide a crate of melons . . . it should be refreshing, to consider the entertainment value of a video special titled *Sinatra—A Man and His Music. . . .*"

But now in this NBC studio in Los Angeles, there was an atmosphere of anticipation and tension because of the uncertainty of the Sinatra voice. The forty-three musicians in Nelson Riddle's orchestra had already arrived and some were up on the white platform warming up. Dwight Hemion, a youthful sandy-haired director who had won praise for his television special on Barbra Streisand, was seated in the glass-enclosed control booth that overlooked the orchestra and stage. The camera crews, technical teams, security guards, Budweiser ad men were also standing between the floor lamps and cameras, waiting, as were a dozen or so ladies who worked as secretaries in other parts of the building but had sneaked away so they could watch this.

A few minutes before eleven o'clock, word spread quickly through the long corridor into the big studio that Sinatra was spotted walking through the parking lot and was on his way, and was looking fine. There seemed great relief among the group that was gathered; but when the lean, sharply dressed figure of the man got closer, and closer, they saw to their dismay that it was not Frank Sinatra. It was his double, Johnny Delgado.

Delgado walks like Sinatra, has Sinatra's build, and from certain facial angles does resemble Sinatra. But he seems a rather shy individual. Fifteen years ago, early in his acting career, Delgado applied for a role in *From Here to Eternity.* He was hired, finding out later that he was to be Sinatra's double. In Sinatra's latest film, *Assault on a Queen,* a story in which Sinatra and some fellow conspirators attempt to hijack the *Queen Mary,* Johnny Delgado doubles for Sinatra in some water scenes; and now, in this NBC studio, his job was to stand under the hot television lights marking Sinatra's spots on the stage for the camera crews.

Five minutes later, the real Frank Sinatra walked in. His face was pale, his blue eyes seemed a bit watery. He had been unable to rid himself of the cold, but he was going to try to sing anyway because the schedule was tight and thousands of dollars were involved at this moment in the assembling of the orchestra and crews and the rental of the studio. But when Sinatra, on his way to his small rehearsal room to warm up his voice, looked into the studio and saw that the stage and orchestra's platform were not close together, as he had specifically requested, his lips tightened and he was obviously very upset. A few moments later, from his rehearsal room, could be heard the pounding of his fist against the top of the piano and the voice of his accompanist, Bill Miller, saying, softly, "Try not to upset yourself, Frank."

Later Jim Mahoney and another man walked in, and there was talk of Dorothy Kilgallen's death in New York earlier that morning. She had been an ardent foe of Sinatra for years, and he became equally uncomplimentary about her in his nightclub act, and now, though she was dead, he did not compromise his feelings. "Dorothy Kilgallen's dead," he repeated, walking out of the room toward the studio. "Well, guess I got to change my whole act."

When he strolled into the studio the musicians all picked up their instruments and stiffened in their seats. Sinatra cleared his throat a few times and then, after rehearsing a few ballads with the orchestra, he sang "Don't Worry About Me" to his satisfaction and, being uncertain of how long his voice could last, suddenly became impatient.

"Why don't we tape this mother?" he called out, looking up toward the glass booth where the director, Dwight Hemion, and his staff were sitting. Their heads seemed to be down, focusing on the control board.

"Why don't we tape this mother?" Sinatra repeated.

The production stage manager, who stands near the camera wearing a headset, repeated Sinatra's words exactly into his line to the control room: "Why don't we tape this mother?"

Hemion did not answer. Possibly his switch was off. It was hard to know because of the obscuring reflections the lights made against the glass booth.

Sinatra and Tony Bennett were dressed formally while dining informally between shows. "I wasn't in the Rat Pack," says Bennett today. "I was in New York, they were out there. I had my singing and painting, and with the hours they kept— **whoa!**—it's just as well I wasn't in that scene."

"Why don't we put on a coat and tie," said Sinatra, then wearing a high-necked yellow pullover, "and tape this…."

Suddenly Hemion's voice came over the sound amplifier, very calmly: "Okay, Frank, would you mind going back over…."

"Yes, I would mind going back," Sinatra snapped.

The silence from Hemion's end, which lasted a second or two, was then again interrupted by Sinatra saying, "When we stop doing things around here the way we did them in 1950, maybe we …" and Sinatra continued to tear into Hemion, condemning as well the lack of modern techniques in putting such shows together; then, possibly not wanting to use his voice unnecessarily, he stopped. And Dwight Hemion, very patient, so patient and calm that one would assume he had not heard anything that Sinatra had just said, outlined the opening part of the show. And Sinatra a few minutes later was reading his opening remarks, words that would follow "Without a Song," off the large idiot-cards being held near the camera. Then, this done, he prepared to do the same thing on camera.

"Frank Sinatra Show, Act I, Page 10, Take I," called a man with a clapboard, jumping in front of the camera—*clap*—then jumping away again.

"Did you ever stop to think," Sinatra began, "what the world would be like without a song? . . . It would be a pretty dreary place. . . . Gives you something to think about, doesn't it? …"

Sinatra stopped.

"Excuse me," he said, adding, "Boy, I need a drink."

They tried it again.

"Frank Sinatra Show, Act I, Page 10, Take 2," yelled the jumping guy with the clapboard.

"Did you ever stop to think what the world would be like without a song? …" Frank Sinatra read it through this time without stopping. Then he rehearsed a few more songs, once or twice interrupting the orchestra when a certain instrumental sound was not quite what he wanted. It was hard to tell how well his voice was going to hold up, for this was early in the show; up to this point, however, everybody in the room seemed pleased, particularly when he sang an old sentimental favorite written more than twenty years ago by Jimmy Van Heusen and Phil Silvers—"Nancy," inspired by the first of Sinatra's three children when she was just a few years old.

If I don't see her each day
I miss her....
Gee what a thrill
Each time I kiss her....

As Sinatra sang these words, though he has sung them hundreds and hundreds of times in the past, it was suddenly obvious to everybody in the studio that something quite special must be going on inside the man, because something quite special was coming out. He was singing now, cold or no cold, with power and warmth, he was letting himself go, the public arrogance was gone, the private side was in this song about the girl who, it is said, understands him better than anybody else, and is the only person in front of whom he can be unashamedly himself.

Nancy is twenty-five. She lives alone, her marriage to singer Tommy Sands having ended in divorce. Her home is in a Los Angeles suburb and she is now making her third film and is recording for her father's record company. She sees him every day; or, if not, he telephones, no matter if it be from Europe or Asia. When Sinatra's singing first became popular on radio, stimulating the swooners, Nancy would listen at home and cry. When Sinatra's first marriage broke up in 1951 and he left home, Nancy was the only child old enough to remember him as a father. She also saw him with Ava Gardner, Juliet Prowse, Mia Farrow, many others, has gone on double dates with him....

She takes the winter
And makes it summer....
Summer could take
Some lessons from her....

Nancy now also sees him visiting at home with his first wife, the former Nancy Barbato, a plasterer's daughter from Jersey City whom he married in 1939 when he was earning $25 a week singing at the Rustic Cabin near Hoboken.

The first Mrs. Sinatra, a striking woman who has never remarried ("When you've been married to Frank Sinatra..."

she once explained to a friend), lives in a magnificent home in Los Angeles with her younger daughter, Tina, who is seventeen. There is no bitterness, only great respect and affection between Sinatra and his first wife, and he has long been welcome in her home and has even been known to wander in at odd hours, stoke the fire, lie on the sofa, and fall asleep. Frank Sinatra can fall asleep anywhere, something he learned when he used to ride bumpy roads with band buses; he also learned at that time, when sitting in a tuxedo, how to pinch the trouser creases in the back and tuck the jacket under and out, and fall asleep perfectly pressed. But he does not ride buses anymore, and his daughter Nancy, who in her younger days felt rejected when he slept on the sofa instead of giving attention to her, later realized that the sofa was one of the few places left in the world where Frank Sinatra could get any privacy, where his famous face would neither be stared at nor cause an abnormal reaction in others. She realized, too, that things normal have always

In Las Vegas, Nancy gave Dad a hug as the actor Yul Brynner looked on. Daughter and father had, by then, traveled a long and sometimes rocky road together to arrive at a good place. As a young girl, Nancy felt rejected if Frank wasn't spending time with her, and, of course, the breakup of her parents' marriage left scars, even though Frank continued to get on well with Nancy's mother. But Nancy was always **the apple of Frank's eye** whether she knew it or not, and eventually she came to know it absolutely. She had, by now, double-dated with Dad and was recording for his record label. She was also about to become a big star in her own right with "These Boots Are Made for Walkin'."

eluded her father: his childhood was one of loneliness and a drive toward attention, and since attaining it he has never again been certain of solitude. Upon looking out the window of a home he once owned in Hasbrouck Heights, New Jersey, he would occasionally see the faces of teen-agers peeking in; and in 1944, after moving to California and buying a home behind a ten-foot fence on Lake Toluca, he discovered that the only way to escape the telephone and other intrusions was to board his paddle boat with a few friends, a card table and a case of beer, and stay afloat all afternoon. But he has tried, insofar as it has been possible, to be like everyone else, Nancy says. He wept on her wedding day, he is very sentimental and sensitive....

"WHAT THE HELL ARE YOU DOING UP there, Dwight?"

Silence from the control booth.

"Got a party or something going on up there, Dwight?"

Sinatra stood on the stage, arms folded, glaring up across the cameras toward Hemion. Sinatra had sung "Nancy" with probably all he had in his voice on this day. The next few numbers contained raspy notes, and twice his voice completely cracked. But now Hemion was in the control booth out of communication; then he was down in the studio walking over to where Sinatra stood. A few minutes later they both left the studio and were on the way up to the control booth. The tape was replayed for Sinatra. He watched only about five minutes of it before he started to shake his head. Then he said to Hemion: "Forget it, just forget it. You're wasting your time. What you got there," Sinatra said, nodding to the singing image of himself on the television screen, "is a man with a cold." Then he left the control booth, ordering that the whole day's performance be scrubbed and future taping postponed until he had recovered.

SOON THE WORD SPREAD LIKE AN EMOTIONAL epidemic down through Sinatra's staff, then fanned out through Hollywood, then was heard across the nation in Jilly's saloon, and also on the other side of the Hudson River in the homes of Frank Sinatra's parents and his other relatives and friends in New Jersey.

When Frank Sinatra spoke with his father on the telephone and said he was feeling awful, the elder Sinatra reported that he was also feeling awful: that his left arm and fist were so stiff with a circulatory condition he could barely use them, adding that the ailment might be the result of having thrown too many left hooks during his days as a bantamweight almost fifty years ago.

Martin Sinatra, a ruddy and tattooed little blue-eyed Sicilian born in Catania, boxed under the name of "Marty O'Brien." In those days, in those places, with the Irish running the lower reaches of city life, it was not uncommon for Italians to wind up with such names. Most of the Italians and Sicilians who migrated to America just prior to the 1900's were poor and uneducated, were excluded from the building-trades unions dominated by the Irish, and were somewhat intimidated by the Irish police, Irish priests, Irish politicians.

One notable exception was Frank Sinatra's mother, Dolly, a large and very ambitious woman who was brought to this country at two months of age by her mother and father, a lithographer from Genoa. In later years Dolly Sinatra, possessing a round red face and blue eyes, was often mistaken for being Irish, and surprised many at the speed with which she swung her heavy handbag at anyone uttering "Wop."

By playing skillful politics with North Jersey's Democratic machine, Dolly Sinatra was to become, in her heyday, a kind of Catherine de Medici of Hoboken's third ward. She could always be counted upon to deliver six hundred votes at election time from her Italian neighborhood, and this was her base of power. When she told one of the politicians that she wanted her husband to be appointed to the Hoboken Fire Department, and was told, "But, Dolly, we don't have an opening," she snapped, "Make an opening."

They did. Years later she requested that her husband be made a captain, and one day she got a call from one of the political bosses that began, "Dolly, congratulations!"

"For what?"

"Captain Sinatra."

"Oh, you finally made him one—thank you very much."

Then she called the Hoboken Fire Department.

"Let me speak to Captain Sinatra," she said. The fireman called Martin Sinatra to the phone, saying, "Marty, I think your wife has gone nuts." When he got on the line, Dolly greeted him:

"Congratulations, Captain Sinatra!"

Dolly's only child, christened Francis Albert Sinatra, was

born and nearly died on December 12, 1915. It was a difficult birth, and during his first moment on earth he received marks he will carry till death—the scars on the left side of his neck being the result of a doctor's clumsy forceps, and Sinatra has chosen not to obscure them with surgery.

After he was six months old, he was reared mainly by his grandmother. His mother had a full-time job as a chocolate dipper with a large firm and was so proficient at it that the firm once offered to send her to the Paris office to train others. While some people in Hoboken remember Frank Sinatra as a lonely child, one who spent many hours on the porch gazing into space, Sinatra was never a slum kid, never in jail, always well-dressed. He had so many pants that some people in Hoboken called him "Slacksey O'Brien."

Dolly Sinatra was not the sort of Italian mother who could be appeased merely by a child's obedience and good appetite. She made many demands on her son, was always very strict. She dreamed of his becoming an aviation engineer. When she discovered Bing Crosby pictures hanging on his bedroom walls one evening, and learned that her son wished to become a singer too, she became infuriated and threw a shoe at him. Later, finding she could not talk him out of it—"he takes after me"—she encouraged his singing.

Many Italo-American boys of his generation were then shooting for the same star—they were strong with song,

In the mid-1960s, Frank rarely saw his son, Frank Jr., who was touring the country as a singer with his own band, living mostly in hotel rooms. But one night in Vegas, father and son were together, and as might be expected, **Senior was giving Junior a pointer** on sartorial splendor (opposite). Frank Jr. felt he fell out of the "inner family circle" after being sent to prep school in 1958 and never fully returned to it. On this page, Frank's third child, Tina, received a peck on the cheek from Dad at a table (certainly one of the good ones) in Vegas.

offer from Tommy Dorsey, who in those days had probably the best band in the country, Sinatra took it; the job paid $125 a week, and Dorsey knew how to feature a vocalist. Yet Sinatra was very depressed at leaving James's band, and the final night with them was so memorable that, twenty years later, Sinatra could recall the details to a friend: " … the bus pulled out with the rest of the boys at about half-past midnight. I'd said good-bye to them all, and it was snowing, I remember. There was nobody around and I stood alone with my suitcase in the snow and watched the taillights disappear. Then the tears started and I tried to run after the bus. There was such spirit and enthusiasm in that band, I hated leaving it.…"

But he did—as he would leave other warm places, too, in search of something more, never wasting time, trying to do it all in one generation, fighting under his own name, defending underdogs, terrorizing top dogs. He threw a punch at a musician who said something anti-Semitic, espoused the

weak with words, not a big novelist among them: no O'Hara, no Bellow, no Cheever, nor Shaw; yet they could communicate bel canto. This was more in their tradition, no need for a diploma; they could, with a song, someday see their names in lights … Perry Como … Frankie Laine … Tony Bennett … Vic Damone … but none could see it better than Frank Sinatra.

Though he sang through much of the night at the Rustic Cabin, he was up the next day singing without a fee on New York radio to get more attention. Later he got a job singing with Harry James's band, and it was there in August of 1939 that Sinatra had his first recording hit—"All or Nothing at All." He became very fond of Harry James and the men in the band, but when he received an

Negro cause two decades before it became fashionable. He also threw a tray of glasses at Buddy Rich when he played the drums too loud.

Sinatra gave away $50,000 worth of gold cigarette lighters before he was thirty, was living an immigrant's wildest dream of America. He arrived suddenly on the scene when DiMaggio was silent, when paisanos were mournful, were quietly defensive about Hitler in their homeland. Sinatra became, in time, a kind of one-man Anti-Defamation League for Italians in America, the sort of organization that would be unlikely for them because, as the theory goes, they rarely agreed on anything, being extreme individualists: fine as soloists, but not so good in a choir; fine as heroes, but not so good in a parade.

When many Italian names were used in describing gangsters on a television show, *The Untouchables,* Sinatra was loud in his disapproval. Sinatra and many thousands of other Italo-Americans were resentful as well when a small-time hoodlum, Joseph Valachi, was brought by Bobby Kennedy into prominence as a Mafia expert, when indeed, from Valachi's testimony on television, he seemed to know less than most waiters on Mulberry Street. Many Italians in Sinatra's circle also regard Bobby Kennedy as something of an Irish cop, more dignified than those in Dolly's day, but no less intimidating. Together with Peter Lawford, Bobby Kennedy is said to have suddenly gotten "cocky" with Sinatra after John Kennedy's election, forgetting the contribution Sinatra had made in both fundraising and in influencing many anti-Irish Italian votes. Lawford and Bobby Kennedy are both suspected of having influenced the late President's decision to stay as a house guest with Bing Crosby instead of Sinatra, as originally planned, a social setback Sinatra may never forget. Peter Lawford has since been drummed out of Sinatra's "summit" in Las Vegas.

"Yes, my son is like me," Dolly Sinatra says, proudly. "You cross him, he never forgets." And while she concedes his power, she quickly points out, "He can't make his mother do anything she doesn't want to do," adding, "Even today, he wears the same brand of underwear I used to buy him."

Today Dolly Sinatra is seventy-one years old, a year or two younger than Martin, and all day long people are knocking on the back door of her large home asking her advice, seeking her influence. When she is not seeing people and not cooking in the kitchen, she is looking after her husband, a silent but stubborn man, and telling him to keep his sore left arm resting on the sponge she has placed on

Frank was right behind parents Dolly and Marty during one of their stays in Las Vegas, where they had an apartment they used in the winter. (Here, the family had just left the Sands; note how much Frank resembled his father.) When back east, the formidable Mrs. Sinatra would talk to her son on the phone once a week from the 16-room Fort Lee, N.J., home he had bought for her and Marty as a 50th wedding anniversary present. **The Sinatra trio** had come a long way from Hoboken.

the armrest of a soft chair. "Oh, he went to some terrific fires, this guy did," Dolly said to a visitor, nodding with admiration toward her husband in the chair.

Though Dolly Sinatra has eighty-seven godchildren in Hoboken, and still goes to that city during political campaigns, she now lives with her husband in a beautiful sixteen-room house in Fort Lee, New Jersey. This home was a gift from their son on their fiftieth wedding anniversary three years ago. The home is tastefully furnished and is filled with a remarkable juxtaposition of the pious and the worldly—photographs of Pope John and Ava Gardner, of Pope Paul and Dean Martin; several statues of saints and holy water, a chair autographed by Sammy Davis, Jr. and bottles of bourbon. In Mrs. Sinatra's jewelry box is a magnificent strand of pearls she had just received from Ava Gardner, whom she liked tremendously as a daughter-in-law and still keeps in touch with and talks about; and hung on the wall is a letter addressed to Dolly and Martin: "The sands of time have turned to gold, yet love continues to unfold like the petals of a rose, in God's garden of life . . . may God love you thru all eternity. I thank Him, I thank you for the being of one. Your loving son, Francis. . . ."

Mrs. Sinatra talks to her son on the telephone about once a week, and recently he suggested that, when visiting Manhattan, she make use of his apartment on East Seventy-second Street on the East River. This is an expensive neighborhood of New York even though there is a small factory on the block, but this latter fact was seized upon by Dolly Sinatra as a means of getting back at her son for some unflattering descriptions of his childhood in Hoboken.

"What—you want me to stay in your apartment, in that dump?" she asked. "You think I'm going to spend the night in that awful neighborhood?"

Frank Sinatra got the point, and said, "Excuse me, Mrs. Fort Lee."

After spending the week in Palm Springs, his cold much better, Frank Sinatra returned to Los Angeles, a lovely city of sun and sex, a Spanish discovery of Mexican misery, a star land of little men and little women sliding in and out of convertibles in tense tight pants.

Sinatra returned in time to see the long-awaited CBS documentary with his family. At about nine p.m. he drove to the home of his former wife, Nancy, and had dinner with her and their two daughters. Their son, whom they rarely see these days, was out of town.

Frank, Jr., who is twenty-two, was touring with a band and moving cross country toward a New York engagement at Basin Street East with The Pied Pipers, with whom Frank Sinatra sang when he was with Dorsey's band in the 1940's. Today Frank Sinatra, Jr., whom his father says he named after Franklin D. Roosevelt, lives mostly in hotels, dines each evening in his nightclub dressing room, and sings until two a.m., accepting graciously, because he has no choice, the inevitable comparisons. His voice is smooth and pleasant, and improving with work, and while he is very respectful of his father, he discusses him with objectivity and in an occasional tone of subdued cockiness.

Concurrent with his father's early fame, Frank, Jr. said, was the creation of a "press-release Sinatra" designed to "set him apart from the common man, separate him from the realities: it was suddenly Sinatra, the electric magnate, Sinatra who is supernormal, not superhuman but supernormal. And here," Frank, Jr. continued, "is the great fallacy, the great bullshit, for Frank Sinatra is normal, is the guy whom you'd meet on a street corner. But this other thing, the supernormal guise, has affected Frank Sinatra as much as anybody who watches one of his television shows, or reads a magazine article about him. . . .

"Frank Sinatra's life in the beginning was so normal," he said, "that nobody would have guessed in 1934 that this little Italian kid with the curly hair would become the giant, the monster, the great living legend. . . . He met my mother one summer on the beach. She was Nancy Barbato, daughter of Mike Barbato, a Jersey City plasterer. And she meets the fireman's son, Frank, one summer day on the beach at Long Branch, New Jersey. Both are Italian, both Roman Catholic, both lower-middle-class summer sweethearts—it is like a million bad movies starring Frankie Avalon. . . .

"They have three children. The first child, Nancy, was the most normal of Frank Sinatra's children. Nancy was a cheerleader, went to summer camp, drove a Chevrolet, had the easiest kind of development centered around the home and family. Next is me. My life with the family is very, very normal up until September of 1958 when, in complete contrast to the rearing of both girls, I am put into a college-preparatory school. I am now away from the inner family circle, and my position within has never been remade to this day. . . . The third child, Tina. And to be dead honest, I really couldn't say what her life is like. . . ."

The CBS show, narrated by Walter Cronkite, began at ten p.m. A minute before that, the Sinatra family, having finished dinner, turned their chairs around and faced the camera, united for whatever disaster might follow. Sinatra's men in other parts of town, in other parts of the nation, were doing the same thing. Sinatra's lawyer, Milton A. Rudin, smoking a cigar, was watching with a keen eye, an alert legal mind. Other sets were watched by Brad Dexter, Jim Mahoney, Ed Pucci; Sinatra's makeup man, "Shotgun" Britton; his New York representative, Henri Gine; his haberdasher, Richard Carroll; his insurance broker, John Lillie; his valet, George Jacobs, a handsome Negro who, when entertaining girls in his apartment, plays records by Ray Charles.

And like so much of Hollywood's fear, the apprehension about the CBS show all proved to be without foundation. It was a highly flattering hour that did not deeply probe, as rumors suggested it would, into Sinatra's love life, or the Mafia, or other areas of his private province. While the documentary was not authorized, wrote Jack Gould in the next day's *New York Times*, "it could have been."

Immediately after the show, the telephones began to ring throughout the Sinatra system conveying words of joy and relief—and from New York came Jilly's telegram: "WE RULE THE WORLD!"

THE NEXT DAY, STANDING IN THE CORRIDOR of the NBC building where he was about to resume taping his show, Sinatra was discussing the CBS show with several of his friends, and he said, "Oh, it was a gas."

"Yeah, Frank, a helluva show."

"But I think Jack Gould was right in *The Times* today," Sinatra said. "There should have been more on the man, not so much on the music. . . ."

They nodded, nobody mentioning the past hysteria in the Sinatra world when it seemed CBS was zeroing in on the man; they just nodded and two of them laughed about Sinatra's apparently having gotten the word "bird" on the show—this being a favorite Sinatra word. He often inquires of his cronies, "How's your bird?"; and when he nearly drowned in Hawaii, he later explained, "Just got a little water on my bird"; and under a large photograph of him holding a whisky bottle, a photo that hangs in the home of an actor friend named Dick Bakalyan, the inscription reads: "Drink, Dickie! It's good for your bird." In the song, "Come Fly with Me," Sinatra sometimes alters the lyrics—" . . . just say the words and we'll take our birds down to Acapulco Bay. . . ."

Ten minutes later Sinatra, following the orchestra, walked into the NBC studio, which did not resemble in the slightest the scene here of eight days ago. On this occasion Sinatra was in fine voice, he cracked jokes between numbers, nothing could upset him. Once, while he was singing "How Can I Ignore the Girl Next Door," standing on the stage next to a tree, a television camera mounted on a vehicle came rolling in too close and plowed against the tree.

"Kee-rist!" yelled one of the technical assistants.

But Sinatra seemed hardly to notice it.

"We've had a slight accident," he said, calmly. Then he began the song all over from the beginning.

When the show was over, Sinatra watched the rerun on the monitor in the control room. He was very pleased, shaking hands with Dwight Hemion and his assistants. Then the whisky bottles were opened in Sinatra's dressing room. Pat Lawford was there, and so were Andy Williams and a dozen others. The telegrams and telephone calls continued to be received from all over the country with praise for the CBS show. There was even a call, Mahoney said, from the CBS producer, Don Hewitt, with whom Sinatra had been so angry a few days before. And Sinatra was still angry, feeling that CBS had betrayed him, though the show itself was not objectionable.

"Shall I drop a line to Hewitt?" Mahoney asked.

"Can you send a fist through the mail?" Sinatra asked.

He has everything, he cannot sleep, he gives nice gifts, he is not happy, but he would not trade, even for happiness, what he is....

He is a piece of our past—but only we have aged, he hasn't ... we are dogged by domesticity, he isn't ... we have compunctions, he doesn't ... it is our fault, not his....

He controls the menus of every Italian restaurant in Los Angeles; if you want North Italian cooking, fly to Milan....

Men follow him, imitate him, fight to be near him ... there is something of the locker room, the barracks about him ... bird ... bird....

He believes you must play it big, wide, expansively— the more open you are, the more you take in, your dimensions deepen, you grow, you become more what you are—bigger, richer....

"He is better than anybody else, or at least they think he is, and he has to live up to it."   —Nancy Sinatra, Jr.

"He is calm on the outside—inwardly a million things are happening to him."   —Dick Bakalyan

"He has an insatiable desire to live every moment to its fullest because, I guess, he feels that right around the corner is extinction."   —Brad Dexter

"All I ever got out of any of my marriages was the two years Artie Shaw financed on an analyst's couch."
          —Ava Gardner

"We weren't mother and son—we were buddies."
          —Dolly Sinatra

"I'm for anything that gets you through the night, be it prayer, tranquilizers or a bottle of Jack Daniel."
          —Frank Sinatra

FRANK SINATRA WAS TIRED OF ALL THE TALK, the gossip, the theory—tired of reading quotes about himself, of hearing what people were saying about him all over town. It had been a tedious three weeks, he said, and now he just wanted to get away, go to Las Vegas, let off some steam. So he hopped in his jet, soared over the California hills, across the Nevada flats, then over miles and miles of desert to The Sands and the Clay-Patterson fight.

On the eve of the fight he stayed up all night and slept through most of the afternoon, though his recorded voice could be heard singing in the lobby of The Sands, in the gambling casino, even in the toilets, being interrupted every few bars however by the paging public address: " ... Telephone call for Mr. Ron Fish, Mr. Ron Fish ... with a ribbon of gold in her hair.... Telephone call for Mr. Herbert Rothstein,

Sinatra slept in many beds, you might say too many. But the house that he considered home in this period was his spread on Wonder Palm Road in Palm Springs, Calif., next to the 17th hole of the Tamarisk Country Club (where, in the 1960s, he could shoot in the mid-80s). Casa Sinatra had two bedrooms, tennis courts, a saltwater pool, a helicopter landing pad, a $100,000 kitchen and two guest houses. It also had, at one point, a sign hanging outside that read: "NEVER MIND THE DOG, **BEWARE OF THE OWNER.**" The pooch in this picture was named Ringo, of all things. Note the bowl overflowing with assorted brands of cigarette packs. On the house's $5,000 worth of hi-fi equipment, Sinatra the stereophile usually listened to classical music, never his own records.

Sinatra made a call from his home under a mounted spread from LIFE that featured a John Dominis photograph (which also serves as the title pages for this book). Sinatra, who got on lousy with most of the press and was usually uncooperative, had a good relationship with the magazine. For the 50th-birthday photo story, he contributed a first-person essay "Me and My Music" to accompany Dominis's pictures. Later, in 1971, he had a ringside seat for the monumental Muhammad Ali–Joe Frazier title bout and wound up taking the cover photograph for the next week's LIFE. (You can read all about it on page 134.) Hence this fellow, whose day job was singing, is one of the elite few to have written and shot for LIFE. The photo here and the one opposite, in which Sinatra confers with film director Jack Donohue, well illustrate Gay Talese's observation that **Sinatra was ever-resplendent.** His casual elegance set a tone, one that was about to be overwhelmed by the studied grunginess of the '60s rock-and-rollers.

Mr. Herbert Rothstein . . . memories of a time so bright, keep me sleepless through dark endless nights. . . ."

Standing around in the lobby of The Sands and other hotels up and down the strip on this afternoon before the fight were the usual prefight prophets: the gamblers, the old champs, the little cigar butts from Eighth Avenue, the sportswriters who knock the big fights all year but would never miss one, the novelists who seem always to be identifying with one boxer or another, the local prostitutes assisted by some talent in from Los Angeles, and also a young brunette in a wrinkled black cocktail dress who was at the bell captain's desk crying, "But I want to speak to Mr. Sinatra."

"He's not here," the bell captain said.

"Won't you put me through to his room?"

"There are no messages going through, Miss," he said, and then she turned, unsteadily, seeming close to tears, and walked through the lobby into the big noisy casino crowded with men interested only in money.

Shortly before seven p.m., Jack Entratter, a big grey-haired man who operates The Sands, walked into the gambling room to tell some men around the blackjack table that Sinatra was getting dressed. He also said that he'd been unable to get front-row seats for everybody, and so some of the men— including Leo Durocher, who had a date, and Joey Bishop, who was accompanied by his wife—would not be able to fit in Frank Sinatra's row but would have to take seats in the third row. When Entratter walked over to tell this to Joey Bishop, Bishop's face fell. He did not seem angry; he merely looked at Entratter with an empty silence, seeming somewhat stunned.

"Joey, I'm sorry," Entratter said when the silence persisted, "but we couldn't get more than six together in the front row."

Bishop still said nothing. But when they all appeared at the fight, Joey Bishop was in the front row, his wife in the third.

The fight, called a holy war between Muslims and Christians, was preceded by the introduction of three balding ex-champions, Rocky Marciano, Joe Louis, Sonny Liston—and then there was "The Star-Spangled Banner" sung by another man from out of the past, Eddie Fisher. It had been more than fourteen years ago, but Sinatra could still remember every detail: Eddie Fisher was then the new king of the baritones, with Billy Eckstine and Guy Mitchell right with him, and Sinatra had been long counted out. One day he remembered walking into a broadcasting studio past dozens of Eddie Fisher fans waiting outside the hall, and when they saw Sinatra they began to jeer, "Frankie, Frankie, I'm swooning, I'm swooning." This was also the time when he was selling only about 30,000 records a year, when he was dreadfully miscast as a funny man on his television show, and when he recorded such disasters as "Mama Will Bark," with Dagmar.

"I growled and barked on the record," Sinatra said, still horrified by the thought. "The only good it did me was with the dogs."

His voice and his artistic judgment were incredibly bad in 1952, but even more responsible for his decline, say his friends, was his pursuit of Ava Gardner. She was the big movie queen then, one of the most beautiful women in the world. Sinatra's daughter Nancy recalls seeing Ava swimming one day in her father's pool, then climbing out of the water with that fabulous body, walking slowly to the fire, leaning over it for a few moments, and then it suddenly seemed that her long dark hair was all dry, miraculously and effortlessly back in place.

With most women Sinatra dates, his friends say, he never knows whether they want him for what he can do for them now—or will do for them later. With Ava Gardner, it was different. He could do nothing for her later. She was on top. If Sinatra learned anything from his experience with her, he possibly learned that when a proud man is down a woman cannot help. Particularly a woman on top.

Nevertheless, despite a tired voice, some deep emotion seeped into his singing during this time. One particular song that is well remembered even now is "I'm a Fool to Want You," and a friend who was in the studio when Sinatra recorded it recalled: "Frank was really worked up that night. He did the song in one take, then turned around and walked out of the studio and that was that…."

Sinatra's manager at that time, a former song plugger named Hank Sanicola, said, "Ava loved Frank, but not the way he loved her. He needs a great deal of love. He wants it twenty-four hours a day, he must have people around—Frank is that kind of guy." Ava Gardner, Sanicola said, "was very insecure. She feared she could not really hold a man … twice he went chasing her to Africa, wasting his own career…."

"Ava didn't want Frank's men hanging around all the time," another friend said, "and this got him mad. With Nancy he used to be able to bring the whole band home with him, and Nancy, the good Italian wife, would never complain—she'd just make everybody a plate of spaghetti."

During a conference with pianist Bill Miller well before showtime, Sinatra accepted a light while Miller stuck to his knitting. Miller was **Sinatra's musical partner** onstage and off- for more than 40 years: a contributor far more unsung but hardly less valuable than the Nelson Riddles and Quincy Joneses of the Sinatra story. Of Sinatra's meticulous attention to his recordings, Miller once said, "He would pick the tunes, and he would even position them on the album."

In 1953, after almost two years of marriage, Sinatra and Ava Gardner were divorced. Sinatra's mother reportedly arranged a reconciliation, but if Ava was willing, Frank Sinatra was not. He was seen with other women. The balance had shifted. Somewhere during this period Sinatra seemed to change from the kid singer, the boy actor in the sailor suit, to a man. Even before he had won the Oscar in 1953 for his role in *From Here to Eternity*, some flashes of his old talent were coming through—in his recording of "The Birth of the Blues," in his Riviera-nightclub appearance that jazz critics enthusiastically praised; and there was also a trend now toward L.P.'s and away from the quick three-minute deal, and Sinatra's concert style would have capitalized on this with or without an Oscar.

In 1954, totally committed to his talent once more, Frank Sinatra was selected *Metronome*'s "Singer of the Year," and later he won the U.P.I. disc-jockey poll, unseating Eddie Fisher—who now, in Las Vegas, having sung "The Star-Spangled Banner," climbed out of the ring, and the fight began.

Floyd Patterson chased Clay around the ring in the first round, but was unable to reach him, and from then on he was Clay's toy, the bout ending in a technical knockout in the twelfth round. A half hour later, nearly everybody had forgotten about the fight and was back at the gambling tables or lining up to buy tickets for the Dean Martin-Sinatra-Bishop nightclub routine on the stage of The Sands. This routine, which includes Sammy Davis, Jr. when he is in town, consists of a few songs and much cutting up, all of it very informal, very special, and rather ethnic—Martin, a drink in hand, asking Bishop: "Did you ever see a Jew jitsu?"; and Bishop, playing a Jewish waiter, warning the two Italians to watch out "because I got my own group—the Matzia."

Then after the last show at The Sands, the Sinatra crowd, which now numbered about twenty—and included Jilly, who had flown in from New York; Jimmy Cannon, Sinatra's favorite sports columnist; Harold Gibbons, a Teamster official expected to take over if Hoffa goes to jail—all got into a line of cars and headed for another club. It was three o'clock. The night was young.

They stopped at The Sahara, taking a long table near the back, and listened to a baldheaded little comedian named Don Rickles, who is probably more caustic than any comic in the country. His humor is so rude, in such bad taste, that it offends no one—it is too offensive to be offensive. Spotting Eddie Fisher among the audience, Rickles proceeded to ridicule him as a lover, saying it was no wonder that he could not handle Elizabeth Taylor; and when two businessmen in the audience acknowledged that they were Egyptian, Rickles cut into them for their country's policy toward Israel; and he strongly suggested that the woman seated at one table with her husband was actually a hooker.

When the Sinatra crowd walked in, Don Rickles could not be more delighted. Pointing to Jilly, Rickles yelled: "How's it feel to be Frank's tractor? ...Yeah, Jilly keeps walking in front of Frank clearing the way." Then, nodding to Durocher, Rickles said, "Stand up, Leo, show Frank how you slide." Then he focused on Sinatra, not failing to mention Mia Farrow, nor that he was wearing a toupee, nor to say that Sinatra was washed up as a singer, and when Sinatra laughed, everybody laughed, and Rickles pointed toward Bishop: "Joey Bishop keeps checking with Frank to see what's funny."

Then, after Rickles told some Jewish jokes, Dean Martin stood up and yelled, "Hey, you're always talking about the Jews, never about the Italians," and Rickles cut him off with, "What do we need the Italians for—all they do is keep the flies off our fish."

Sinatra laughed, they all laughed, and Rickles went on this way for nearly an hour until Sinatra, standing up, said, "All right, com'on, get this thing over with. I gotta go."

"Shaddup and sit down!" Rickles snapped. "I've had to listen to you sing...."

"Who do you think you're talking to?" Sinatra yelled back.

"Dick Haymes," Rickles replied, and Sinatra laughed again, and then Dean Martin, pouring a bottle of whisky over his head, entirely drenching his tuxedo, pounded the table.

"Who would ever believe that staggering would make a star?" Rickles said, but Martin called out, "Hey, I wanna make a speech."

"Shaddup."

"No, Don, I wanna tell ya," Dean Martin persisted, "that I think you're a great performer."

"Well, thank you, Dean," Rickles said, seeming pleased.

"But don't go by me," Martin said, plopping down into his seat, "I'm drunk."

"I'll buy that," Rickles said.

BY FOUR A.M. FRANK SINATRA LED THE GROUP out of The Sahara, some of them carrying their glasses of whisky with them, sipping it along the sidewalk and in the cars; then, returning to The Sands, they walked into the gambling casino. It was still packed with people, the roulette wheels spinning, the crapshooters screaming in the far corner.

Frank Sinatra, holding a shot glass of bourbon in his left hand, walked through the crowd. He, unlike some of his friends, was perfectly pressed, his tuxedo tie precisely pointed, his shoes unsmudged. He never seems to lose his dignity, never lets his guard completely down no matter how much he has drunk, nor how long he has been up. He never sways when he walks, like Dean Martin, nor does he ever dance in the aisles or jump up on tables, like Sammy Davis.

A part of Sinatra, no matter where he is, is never there. There is always a part of him, though sometimes a small part, that remains Il Padrone. Even now, resting his shot glass on the blackjack table, facing the dealer, Sinatra stood a bit back from the table, not leaning against it. He reached under his tuxedo jacket into his trouser pocket and came up with a thick but clean wad of bills. Gently he peeled off a one-hundred-dollar bill and placed it on the green-felt table. The dealer dealt him two cards. Sinatra called for a third card, overbid, lost the hundred.

Without a change of expression, Sinatra put down a second hundred-dollar bill. He lost that. Then he put down a

The preshow ritual was precise. There would be tea to sooth Sinatra's pipes. There would be a last-minute conversation with the orchestra leader. There would be the doffing of the patent leather loafers that Sinatra called his "Mary Janes." He would check that the mints were in the inside jacket pocket, the folded tissues were in the outer left pocket. (He also carried, always, a money clip heavy with new bills—no wallet and no credit cards—and precisely one house key, which opened all his homes.) The handkerchief, which Sinatra folded himself **just so,** was made of the finest linen.

third, and lost that. Then he placed two one-hundred-dollar bills on the table and lost those. Finally, putting his sixth hundred-dollar bill on the table, and losing it, Sinatra moved away from the table, nodding to the man, and announcing, "Good dealer."

The crowd that had gathered around him now opened up to let him through. But a woman stepped in front of him, handing him a piece of paper to autograph. He signed it and then he said, "Thank you."

In the rear of The Sands' large dining room was a long table reserved for Sinatra. The dining room was fairly empty at this hour, with perhaps two dozen other people in the room, including a table of four unescorted young ladies sitting near Sinatra. On the other side of the room, at another long table, sat seven men shoulder-to-shoulder against the wall, two of them wearing dark glasses, all of them eating quietly, speaking hardly a word, just sitting and eating and missing nothing.

The Sinatra party, after getting settled and having a few more drinks, ordered something to eat. The table was about the same size as the one reserved for Sinatra whenever he is at Jilly's in New York; and the people seated around this table in Las Vegas were many of the same people who are often seen with Sinatra at Jilly's or at a restaurant in California, or in Italy, or in New Jersey, or wherever Sinatra happens to be. When Sinatra sits to dine, his trusted friends are close; and no matter where he is, no matter how elegant the place may be, there is something of the neighborhood showing because Sinatra, no matter how far he has come, is still something of the boy from the neighborhood—only now he can take his neighborhood with him.

In some ways, this quasi-family affair at a reserved table in a public place is the closest thing Sinatra now has to home life. Perhaps, having had a home and left it, this approximation is as close as he cares to come; although this does not seem precisely so because he speaks with such warmth about his family, keeps in close touch with his first wife, and insists that she make no decision without first consulting him. He is always eager to place his furniture or other mementos of himself in her home or his daughter

Nancy's, and he also is on amiable terms with Ava Gardner. When he was in Italy making *Von Ryan's Express,* they spent some time together, being pursued wherever they went by the paparazzi. It was reported then that the paparazzi had made Sinatra a collective offer of $16,000 if he would pose with Ava Gardner; Sinatra was said to have made a counter offer of $32,000 if he could break one paparazzi arm and leg.

While Sinatra is often delighted that he can be in his home completely without people, enabling him to read and think without interruption, there are occasions when he finds himself alone at night, and not by choice. He may have dialed a half-dozen women, and for one reason or another they are all unavailable. So he will call his valet, George Jacobs.

"I'll be coming home for dinner tonight, George."

"How many will there be?"

"Just myself," Sinatra will say. "I want something light, I'm not very hungry."

George Jacobs is a twice-divorced man of thirty-six who resembles Billy Eckstine. He has traveled all over the world with Sinatra and is devoted to him. Jacobs lives in a comfortable bachelor's apartment off Sunset Boulevard around the corner from Whiskey à Go Go, and he is known around town for the assortment of frisky California girls he has as friends—a few of whom, he concedes, were possibly drawn to him initially because of his closeness to Frank Sinatra.

When Sinatra arrives, Jacobs will serve him dinner in the dining room. Then Sinatra will tell Jacobs that he is free to go home. If Sinatra, on such evenings, should ask Jacobs to stay longer, or to play a few hands of poker, he would be happy to do so. But Sinatra never does.

THIS WAS HIS SECOND NIGHT IN LAS VEGAS, and Frank Sinatra sat with friends in The Sands' dining room until nearly eight a.m. He slept through much of the day, then flew back to Los Angeles, and on the following morning he was driving his little golf cart through the Paramount Pictures movie lot. He was scheduled to complete two final scenes with the sultry blonde actress, Virna Lisi, in the film *Assault on a Queen.* As he maneuvered the little vehicle up the road between the big studio buildings, he spotted Steve Rossi who, with his comedy partner Marty Allen, was making a film in an adjoining studio with Nancy Sinatra.

"Hey, Dag," he yelled to Rossi, "stop kissing Nancy."

"It's part of the film, Frank," Rossi said, turning as he walked.

"In the garage?"

"It's my Dago blood, Frank."

"Well, cool it," Sinatra said, winking, then cutting his golf cart around a corner and parking it outside a big drab building within which the scenes for *Assault* would be filmed.

"Where's the fat director?" Sinatra called out, striding into the studio that was crowded with dozens of technical assistants and actors all gathered around cameras. The director, Jack Donohue, a large man who has worked with Sinatra through twenty-two years on one production or other, has had headaches with this film. The script had been chopped, the actors seemed restless, and Sinatra had become bored. But now there were only two scenes left—a short one to be filmed in the pool, and a longer and passionate one featuring Sinatra and Virna Lisi to be shot on a simulated beach.

The pool scene, which dramatizes a situation where Sinatra and his hijackers fail in their attempt to sack the *Queen Mary*, went quickly and well. After Sinatra had been kept in the water shoulder-high for a few minutes, he said, "Let's move it, fellows—it's cold in this water, and I've just gotten over one cold."

So the camera crews moved in closer, Virna Lisi splashed next to Sinatra in the water, and Jack Donohue yelled to his assistants operating the fans, "Get the waves going," and another man gave the command, "Agitate!" and Sinatra broke out in song, "Agitate in rhythm," then quieted down just before the cameras started to roll.

Frank Sinatra was on the beach in the next situation, supposedly gazing up at the stars, and Virna Lisi was to approach him, toss one of her shoes near him to announce her presence, then sit near him and prepare for a passionate session. Just before beginning, Miss Lisi made a practice

toss of her shoe toward the prone figure of Sinatra sprawled on the beach. As she tossed her shoe, Sinatra called out, "Hit me in my bird and I'm going home."

Virna Lisi, who understands little English and certainly none of Sinatra's special vocabulary, looked confused, but everybody behind the camera laughed. She threw the shoe toward him. It twirled in the air, landed on his stomach.

Sinatra was always careful—and astute—about his appearance. Talese writes in his profile of the care and attention paid to the hairpiece, and the same meticulousness was always on display in the wardrobe. This had long been the case. As a young man Sinatra had always favored bow ties because he felt they framed his big smile and handsome face. During these years he also wore pleated trousers, which would make his skinny body seem heftier. By the 1960s he was often seen in slenderizing suits of dark blue, black or charcoal gray. (He despised brown, a near cousin to his favorite color, orange.) In his work clothes, the tuxedo, he was careful to show just the right amount of shirt cuff. His cuff links, of which he had many, were **luxurious but understated items,** most bought from a jeweler in Florida whom he liked.

"Well, that's about three inches too high," he announced. She again was puzzled by the laughter behind the camera.

Then Jack Donohue had them rehearse their lines, and Sinatra, still very charged from the Las Vegas trip, and anxious to get the cameras rolling, said, "Let's try one." Donohue, not certain that Sinatra and Lisi knew their lines well enough, nevertheless said okay, and an assistant with a clapboard called, "419, Take I," and Virna Lisi approached with the shoe, tossed it at Frank lying on the beach. It fell short of his thigh, and Sinatra's right eye raised almost imperceptibly, but the crew got the message, smiled.

"What do the stars tell you tonight?" Miss Lisi said, delivering her first line, and sitting next to Sinatra on the beach.

"The stars tell me tonight I'm an idiot," Sinatra said, "a

gold-plated idiot to get mixed up in this thing...."

"Cut," Donohue said. There were some microphone shadows on the sand, and Virna Lisi was not sitting in the proper place near Sinatra.

"419, Take 2," the clapboard man called.

Miss Lisi again approached, threw the shoe at him, this time falling short—Sinatra exhaling only slightly—and she said, "What do the stars tell you tonight?"

"The stars tell me I'm an idiot, a gold-plated idiot to get mixed up in this thing...." Then, according to the script, Sinatra was to continue, "...do you know what we're getting into? The minute we step on the deck of the *Queen Mary*, we've just tattooed ourselves," but Sinatra, who often improvises on lines, recited them: "...do you know what we're getting into? The minute we step on the deck of that mother's-ass ship...."

"No, no," Donohue interrupted, shaking his head, "I don't think that's right."

The cameras stopped, some people laughed, and Sinatra looked up from his position in the sand as if he had been unfairly interrupted.

"I don't see why that can't work," he began, but Richard Conte, standing behind the camera, yelled, "It won't play in London."

Donohue pushed his hand through his thinning grey hair and said, but not really in anger, "You know, that scene was pretty good until somebody blew the line...."

"Yeah," agreed the cameraman, Billy Daniels, his head popping out from around the camera, "it was a pretty good piece...."

"Watch your language," Sinatra cut in. Then Sinatra, who has a genius for figuring out ways of not reshooting scenes, suggested a way in which the film could be used and the "mother" line could be recorded later. This met with approval. Then the cameras were rolling again, Virna Lisi was leaning toward Sinatra in the sand, and then he pulled her down close to him. The camera now moved in for a close-up of their faces, ticking away for a few long seconds, but Sinatra and Lisi did not stop kissing, they just lay together in the sand wrapped in one another's arms, and

then Virna Lisi's left leg just slightly began to rise a bit, and everybody in the studio now watched in silence, not saying anything until Donohue finally called out:

"If you ever get through, let me know. I'm running out of film."

Then Miss Lisi got up, straightened out her white dress, brushed back her blonde hair and touched her lipstick, which was smeared. Sinatra got up, a little smile on his lips, and headed for his dressing room.

Passing an older man who stood near a camera, Sinatra asked, "How's your Bell & Howell?"

The older man smiled.

"It's fine, Frank."

"Good."

In his dressing room Sinatra was met by an automobile designer who had the plans for Sinatra's new custom-built model to replace the $25,000 Ghia he has been driving for the last few years. He also was awaited by his secretary, Tom Conroy, who had a bag full of fan mail, including a letter from New York's Mayor John Lindsay; and by Bill Miller, Sinatra's pianist, who would rehearse some of the songs that would be recorded later in the evening for Sinatra's newest album, *Moonlight Sinatra*.

While Sinatra does not mind hamming it up a bit on a movie set, he is extremely serious about his recording sessions; as he explained to a British writer, Robin Douglas-Home: "Once you're on that record singing, it's you and you alone. If it's bad and gets you criticized, it's you who's to blame—no one else. If it's good, it's also you. With a film it's never like that; there are producers and scriptwriters, and hundreds of men in offices and the thing is taken right out of your hands. With a record, you're it...."

But now the days are short
I'm in the autumn of the year
And now I think of my life
As vintage wine
From fine old kegs....

It no longer matters what song he is singing, or who wrote the words—they are all his words, his sentiments, they are chapters from the lyrical novel of his life.

Sinatra felt too few singers knew what to do with the microphone. It was, he wrote in LIFE back in 1965, "their instrument—instead of playing a saxophone, they're **playing a microphone."** And there was a visual component to its proper use as well, especially when in Sinatra's capable hands. He liked a black microphone that would not contrast with his dinner jacket, and he moved it about fluidly. One might think of a conductor with a baton, but Sinatra had a more seductive metaphor: "It's like a geisha girl uses her fan."

Life is a beautiful thing
As long as I hold the string....

When Frank Sinatra drives to the studio, he seems to dance out of the car across the sidewalk into the front door; then, snapping his fingers, he is standing in front of the orchestra in an intimate, airtight room, and soon he is dominating every man, every instrument, every sound wave. Some of the musicians have accompanied him for twenty-five years, have gotten old hearing him sing "You Make Me Feel So Young."

When his voice is on, as it was tonight, Sinatra is in ecstasy, the room becomes electric, there is an excitement that spreads through the orchestra and is felt in the control booth where a dozen men, Sinatra's friends, wave at him from behind the glass. One of the men is the Dodgers' pitcher, Don Drysdale ("Hey, Big D," Sinatra calls out, "hey, baby!"); another is the professional golfer Bo Wininger; there are also numbers of pretty women standing in the booth behind the engineers, women who smile at Sinatra and softly move their bodies to the mellow mood of his music:

Will this be moon love
Nothing but moon love
Will you be gone when the dawn
Comes stealing through....

After he is finished, the record is played back on tape, and Nancy Sinatra, who has just walked in, joins her father near the front of the orchestra to hear the playback. They listen silently, all eyes on them, the king, the princess; and when the music ends there is applause from the control booth, Nancy smiles, and her father snaps his fingers and says, kicking a foot, "Ooba-deeba-boobe-do!"

Then Sinatra calls to one of his men. "Hey, Sarge, think I can have a half-a-cup of coffee?"

Sarge Weiss, who had been listening to the music, slowly gets up.

"Didn't mean to wake ya, Sarge," Sinatra says, smiling.

Then Weiss brings the coffee, and Sinatra looks at it, smells it, then announces, "I thought he'd be nice to me, but it's really coffee...."

There are more smiles, and then the orchestra prepares for the next number. And one hour later, it is over.

The musicians put their instruments into their cases, grab their coats, and begin to file out, saying good-night to Sinatra. He knows them all by name, knows much about them personally, from their bachelor days, through their divorces, through their ups and downs, as they know him. When a French-horn player, a short Italian named Vincent DeRosa, who has played with Sinatra since The Lucky Strike "Hit Parade" days on radio, strolled by, Sinatra reached out to hold him for a second.

"Vicenzo," Sinatra said, "how's your little girl?"

"She's fine, Frank."

"Oh, she's not a little girl anymore," Sinatra corrected himself, "she's a big girl now."

"Yes, she goes to college now. U.S.C."

"That's great."

"She's also got a little talent, I think, Frank, as a singer."

Sinatra was silent for a moment, then said, "Yes, but it's very good for her to get her education first, Vicenzo."

Vincent DeRosa nodded.

"Yes, Frank," he said, and then he said, "Well, good-night, Frank."

"Good-night, Vicenzo."

After the musicians had all gone, Sinatra left the recording room and joined his friends in the corridor. He was going to go out and do some drinking with Drysdale, Wininger, and a few other friends, but first he walked to the other end of the corridor to say good-night to Nancy, who was getting her coat and was planning to drive home in her own car.

After Sinatra had kissed her on the cheek, he hurried to join his friends at the door. But before Nancy could leave the studio, one of Sinatra's men, Al Silvani, a former prizefight manager, joined her.

"Are you ready to leave yet, Nancy?"

"Oh, thanks, Al," she said, "but I'll be all right."

"Pope's orders," Silvani said, holding his hands up, palms out.

Only after Nancy had pointed to two of her friends who would escort her home, and only after Silvani recognized them as friends, would he leave.

THE REST OF THE MONTH WAS BRIGHT AND balmy. The record session had gone magnificently, the film was finished, the television shows were out of the way, and now Sinatra was in his Ghia driving out to his office to begin coordinating his latest projects. He had an engagement at The Sands, a new spy film called *The Naked Runner* to be shot in England, and a couple more albums to do in the immediate months ahead. And within a week he would be fifty years old....

Life is a beautiful thing
As long as I hold the string
I'd be a silly so-and-so
If I should ever let go....

Frank Sinatra stopped his car. The light was red. Pedestrians passed quickly across his windshield but, as usual, one did not. It was a girl in her twenties. She remained at the curb staring at him. Through the corner of his left eye he could see her, and he knew, because it happens almost every day, that she was thinking, It looks like him, but is it?

Just before the light turned green, Sinatra turned toward her, looked directly into her eyes waiting for the reaction he knew would come. It came and he smiled. She smiled and he was gone.

You're back in New York, at the corner of 52nd and 8th—now a business-lunch mecca. Here, late on a sad night in 1979, it was quitting time. Jilly's, the nightspot run by Frank's friend since the '50s, was closing its doors for good. The reason: Jilly wanted to be with Frank more often, and Frank was more often in Palm Springs those days. So Jilly was bound for California to open Jilly's West.

You see, New York just wasn't working anymore. In New York, late '70s, the idea of a nightspot was CBGB or the Mudd Club. Even Studio 54, where at least the people dressed up, well, even that just wasn't Sinatra's scene.

The twilight of a god: Sinatra in the back room of Jilly's, in his special chair, talking about … what? About Sammy's problems with cocaine, which have gotten him exiled again? About marijuana, which he disapproves of, even if it's Mia smoking it? About the clothes people are wearing? About the music they're playing, Sinatra griping there are too few "deejays brave enough to give me equal time in Beatle Land"?

There was a lot going on in those days, but Sinatra wasn't in on it. Oh, he tried. He recorded Beatles songs and actually made something out of "Something," but for years he called it a great Lennon-McCartney tune, when actually it was penned by George Harrison. Sinatra had his hits—"That's Life," "My Way"—but they were hardly great songs, and something just wasn't *right*. It was such a strange time; Sinatra's equilibrium was way out of whack. But he'd get through this. He'd gotten through worse. Keep the faith, baby.

The paparazzi loved it: In 1966 **the swinger married the flower child.** Sinatra was 50, Mia Farrow was 21, but on the eve of the ceremony, Sinatra said to his daughter Nancy, "We have to try." They did, for 16 hectic months; on this good night (above) they were partying at the Sands. Farrow, who would go on to build a fascinating *résumé d'amour*—Frank, André Previn, Woody Allen—always remembered Sinatra fondly: "TV in bed, our puppies, his incredible sweetness, the purity of his feelings. His smile. Our ages finally mattered. I was too ill at ease with his remoteness and unable to fathom his complexities." Mia's sentiments were shared by the other Mrs. Sinatras. Although he had trouble staying friendly with his wives, Frank got along famously with ex-wives, particularly Nancy. Raquel Welch had a theory: "She knew him when he was nothing, and he trusted her absolutely." Maybe that was it. Sinatra said that he sang "Nancy with the Laughing Face" for two women, a daughter and her mother. "It's sort of a family song."

Frank took **his lovely young bride** for a whirl across the floor at the Sands in October 1966.

CHARLES BONNAY

Above: The photo that launched a thousand questions, many of them from federal investigators. The obvious one was why Sinatra, after decades of denying mob links, would pose backstage at the Westchester Premier Theater with (top, fifth from left) Carlo Gambino and his friends. Politeness was Sinatra's explanation under oath. He'd been told that "Mr. Gambino had arrived with his granddaughter, whose name happened to be Sinatra . . . and they'd like to take a picture. I said, 'Fine.' They came in and they took a picture of the little girl, and before I realized what happened, there were approximately eight or nine men standing around me. . . . **I didn't even know their names,** let alone their backgrounds."

Opposite: The things he would try! Sinatra recorded Paul Simon's "Mrs. Robinson" in 1969 as a swinging, big-band showstopper, customizing the line "Jesus loves you more than you will know" as "*Jilly* loves you more than you will know." **Wo, wo, wo, indeed.** He covered Sonny and Cher's "Bang Bang (My Baby Shot Me Down)," which had been written by his Palm Springs pal Sonny Bono. Not since "Mama Will Bark" had there been such a jaw-droppingly absurd example of Sinatra vocalese (the arrangement was painful, too). He recorded an entire album of folk-songy stuff called *Cycles*—George Harrison checked out the sessions— for which critic and ultimate Sinatra defender Will Friedwald suggested an alternative title: *Somethin' Even More Stupid.* But Sinatra wasn't a stupid man, and he knew when things didn't feel right. In 1971 he announced his retirement—setting the stage for a record-breaking string of comebacks.

Our 20 Desert Island Albums

Frank Sinatra Sings for Only the Lonely

Songs for Swingin' Lovers!

In the Wee Small Hours

Francis Albert Sinatra & Antonio Carlos Jobim

Come Fly with Me

Come Dance with Me!

A Duo of Dogs Come Swing with Me

Ring-a-Ding Ding!

Duets Frank Sinatra and Tommy Dorsey: Greatest Hits

Duets II Sing and Dance with Frank Sinatra

Songs for Young Lovers

A Swingin' Affair

Sinatra: A Man and His Music

Nice 'n' Easy

Sinatra-Basie at the Sands

Sinatra and Sextet: Live in Paris

Close to You

Swing Easy

Moonlight Sinatra

A Jolly Christmas with Frank Sinatra

19 Big Awards

Academy Awards (3—2 for special honors)

Grammy Awards (11)

Emmy Award (1965)

Peabody Award (1965)

Presidential Medal of Freedom (1985)

Kennedy Center Honor (1986)

NAACP Lifetime Achievement Award (1987)

The drive from L.A. to Palm Springs

is a lonely one. It gives you time to

think. Today, as you drive it, you

think of Sinatra and the extra-

ordinary road he traveled to get

from Hoboken, N.J., to here. "The

memory of all that," he sings on the

CD player. "No, no, they can't take

that away from me." Suddenly, up

pops Palm Springs. You're hungry.

You pull into Livreri for some pasta.

PHIL STERN/CPI

Livreri: Finally, a Sinatra joint that still exists, and in its way a perfect memorial. In the back, a pseudo-Sinatra works over the standards as couples snuggle. This is the Sands writ very small. Out front, it's the Clam Broth House all over: Sinatra photos on the walls bear best wishes from the man himself. Soft songs float above the bustle, each and every one genuine Sinatra. Beautiful song after beautiful song. It seems like they'll play on forever. And they will.

The beautiful Barbara Marx, not yet divorced from Zeppo, was at Sinatra's side on a visit to the Nixon White House in November 1972 (opposite) and on the dating circuit (this page) for a good long while. She became **the singer's fourth wife** in 1976, then watched her husband evolve from mere icon to American institution.

Talk about heavyweights: Ali, Frazier, Mailer, Sinatra. Famous pugilists all (a couple of them famous in other realms as well), and they converged on Madison Square Garden on March 8, 1971, to see if Ali, returning to the ring after a four-year exile, could steal Frazier's crown. He couldn't, on this night—but the fight was a beauty, and there to record it were writer Norman Mailer, working on a two-day deadline for LIFE, and **cub photog** Frank Sinatra. As Ralph Graves explained in his Editor's Note: "Six years ago staff writer Tommy Thompson and photographer John Dominis were doing a story on Frank Sinatra. Sinatra was fascinated by Dominis' equipment and admitted he had been interested in taking pictures for 20 years. Shortly before the fight Tommy learned that Sinatra had wangled himself a ringside seat and was going to take pictures with a battery of cameras. Tommy went to work wangling Sinatra into letting us have a look at his film. We didn't expect to get anything the professional photographers didn't have, but it might be worth inspecting. Indeed, Sinatra wound up getting the cover, a memorable full-spread picture (yes, he held his camera at that angle on purpose) and two other shots in our story. We are offering him a job."

Dean, Sammy and Frank reunited for a concert tour in 1988; Sinatra was hoping the effort would bolster the spirits of the disconsolate, downward-spiraling Dino, whose 35-year-old son had just been killed. (Dean Paul's Air Force Phantom jet had crashed into the very same California mountain that a decade earlier had claimed Sinatra's beloved mother, Dolly, in a plane crash.) Martin, at 70, was reluctant to do the tour and would later consider it the "biggest mistake of my life." **The Together Again Tour** was to hit 29 cities, and all dates sold out in advance. Martin started out okay, but his performance soon turned sloppy, even embarrassing. Sinatra blew up; Martin walked out. He checked into the hospital, and the official word was that a kidney ailment had sidelined him. But Sinatra told Larry King: "You can't put a gun to his head. He just didn't want to do it." Martin was replaced by Liza Minnelli, and the renamed Ultimate Event Tour drew standing ovations the rest of the year, as did Sinatra's 1992 dates with Minnelli and Shirley MacLaine, as did the many solo shows he performed around the world before taking a final bow in Palm Springs in 1995 (last song: "The Best Is Yet to Come").

Sammy was hit with throat cancer the year after the reunion tour and died the year after that, at 64. Ava Gardner also died in 1990, at 67. In 1992, Jilly Rizzo was killed in a car crash on his 75th birthday. Martin died in 1995, at 78. At that time, Sinatra said, "I'm next. I ain't scared, either. Everybody I ever knew is already over there."

The White House that Bobby Kennedy once made off-limits to Sinatra flung open its doors for the man when **the Reagans were in power.** This photo first ran in LIFE and greatly displeased White House deputy chief of staff Michael Deaver: He felt, as RFK had, that Sinatra's "connections" made him too hot.

139

In later years he drew pleasure from **the quieter things.** He loved dogs, had as many as eight at one time and took daily walks with them. Once, he saved a King Charles spaniel from the pound and surprised Barbara with it at Christmas. The dog slept each night at the foot of their bed.

141

It's 1998, 10 years ago. Tony Bennett is sitting in the upstairs room at Teodora, an Italian restaurant on 57th Street, just off Lexington Avenue, in New York City. It is a few months before Sinatra, who is known to be ill, will pass away, and Bennett is reminiscing fondly about his friend. He sips red wine and considers what the world will be like without Sinatra. For himself, it will be a lesser place, Bennett says. But for those who loved Sinatra from afar, "there will be no void." He gazes out the window and endeavors to explain.

"You see, it's not that way with musicians. They leave behind the music, which will live forever. We'll never lose Sinatra."

Bennett pauses, then continues: "I'm reminded of the day Gershwin died. One of his best friends was told about it, and he just stared. 'Gershwin died,' he said. 'Gershwin died?'

"And then he said, 'I don't have to believe that.'"